Debbie Yates
'82

EP Sport Series

* All about Judo
* Badminton
* Basketball
  Competitive Swimming
* Conditioning for Sport
  Cricket
  Field Athletics
* Football
* Golf
  Hockey for Men and Women
  Improve your Riding
  Learning to Swim
  Men's Gymnastics
  Modern Riding
* Netball
* Orienteering
  Rock Climbing
  Sailing
* Snooker
* Squash Rackets
  Start Motor Cruising
* Table Tennis
* Tennis up to Tournament
    Standard
* Track Athletics
  Underwater Swimming
  Volleyball
  Wildwater Canoeing

At the time of publication of this edition the asterisked titles are available in paperback as well as hardback

ep EP PUBLISHING LIMITED
1977

ep sport

women's gymnastics

jill coulton
B.A.G.A. Senior Coach

Acknowledgements

The author and publishers would like to thank the following gymnasts for their help in the production of this book:
Julie Barker, Susan Buffham, Tracey Coulton, Jackie Desort, Gail Fortune, Kathryn Gelder, Joan Gillies, Denise Hardy, Beverley Harfield, Ann Hurford, Lynda Jacobs, Susan Limbach, Kylie Morgan, Anne Parkinson, Angela Porter, Carol Scott, Helen Sheals and Loraine Stocks.
Photographs on pp. 89, 95, 98 and 111 by Colorsport; those on pp. 2, 35 and 59 by Tony Duffy. All other photographs, and the cover photograph, were taken by Graham Mathers.

ISBN 0 7158 0592 4 (cased edition)
ISBN 0 7158 0702 1 (limp edition)

Published by EP Publishing Ltd, East Ardsley, Wakefield, West Yorkshire 1977

Reprinted 1979

Text set in 10/11 pt Monophoto Univers, printed by photo-lithography, and bound in Great Britain by G. Beard & Son Ltd, Brighton

Foreword

It is with a great deal of pleasure that I write a foreword to this book, *EP Sport Women's Gymnastics.* I have known the author, Jill Coulton, for over 20 years and know of no-one whose experience, both as a competitor and as a coach, better qualifies them to write such a book.

An Olympic competitor and international gymnast herself, Jill has had 17 years experience coaching girls at all levels and many a British international gymnast and British gymnastic champion owes a great debt to her skill and dedication.

Today, in addition to her role as a Senior Coach of the British Amateur Gymnastics Association, she is Britain's leading women's coach for Sports Acrobatics, and her coaching commitments are greater than ever before. That she has found the time to write this book is a further indication of her total dedication to the sport.

The book is clearly and simply written and extremely well illustrated. I unhesitatingly recommend it to every gymnast and coach, confident that it will improve their technical knowledge of the sport and increase the pleasure and joy they will find through the pursuit of gymnastic perfection.

G. WHITELEY
Member of the Executive
Committee
Fédération Internationale de
Gymnastique
1977

CONTENTS

Introduction

Gymnastics for women and girls is a very exciting and demanding sport, as the first-class gymnast requires not only courage and endurance, but also poise, suppleness and an artistic creativity.

It is my experience that these attributes rarely occur together naturally in one individual, and the road to the top is therefore a long, arduous one, requiring patience from gymnast and coach and a determination to reach perfection at all stages of development.

If perfection is sought from the beginning by both gymnast and coach, we will prepare much better gymnasts to represent our country.

Although ambition and determination to reach the top are essential qualities of the competitive gymnast, gymnastics is a very satisfying and enjoyable activity whatever standard is achieved, and it is an excellent way of developing a fit body. The aim of this book is to give gymnast and coach a knowledge of basic gymnastics to a point where simple voluntary exercises can be performed on all pieces of apparatus.

Safety in the Gym

Gymnastics is a very disciplined sport, and discipline means safety. It is most important that basic safety rules are established at a very early stage.

- A great deal of thought must always be given to the layout of the gym; for example, landings from the vault must not interfere with landings from the beam or asymmetric bars.
- The gymnastic equipment must be checked every time it is used.
- Mats must be placed round all equipment in a sensible manner, and not in such a way that landings are on the edge of a mat or the joining of two mats.
- All gymnastics clubs should have an up-to-date first-aid kit. It must be checked regularly and stocks replenished when necessary.
- Movement from one piece of apparatus to another must always be under control, so that there is no interference with a vaulting run, beam dismount, etc.
- Gymnasts must be adequately supervised at all times, and never left alone in the gymnasium.
- Gymnasts can assist coaches by ensuring that they do not attempt a skill of which they are unsure when the coach is occupied elsewhere in the gym.

Equipment

Details of equipment used in competitive women's gymnastics are given on p. 9. Gymnasts and coaches should be fully aware of the correct dimensions of the equipment, even though it may not be possible for the individual club to have all the required apparatus. For example, if the club

Floor: 12 × 12 m
Beam: length—500 cm depth—16 cm width—10 cm height—Seniors, 120 cm Heights for Juniors vary and are set by the organising body of each competition
Asymmetric Bars: height—high bar, 230 cm low bar, 150 cm
Vaulting Horse: height—120 cm for Seniors. Heights for Juniors vary and are set by the organising body of each competition
Board: FIG (Federation of International Gymnastics) competition springboard

does not have a 12 × 12 m mat for the floor, this dimension must still be borne in mind when designing the pattern of the floor exercise.

Clothing

In competition the gymnast is required to wear a leotard which must be made of non-transparent cloth. Footwear is optional, but thick socks or gymnastic shoes together with a track suit are an important part of the gymnast's wardrobe in order that she can keep warm during competitions and whilst training.

The choice of leotard and track suit is left to the individual or club, although if the competition is a team event members of the team must dress alike. One of the exciting things about gymnastics today is the wonderful variety of colour and style in leotards and track suits worn by gymnasts throughout the world.

The gymnast should make every effort to present herself well at all times, both at training sessions and, especially, at competitions. Leotards must be a good fit, hair tidy and footwear, if worn, clean and neat. This will not only give a good impression to the judge or coach but will give a feeling of well-being to the gymnast herself and so improve her performance.

Content of the Gymnastic Exercise

The gymnastic exercise on all four pieces of apparatus is marked out of 10. The Federation of International Gymnastics has devised a code of points which explains fully how the mark of 10 is arrived at. Items taken into account in the evaluation of the exercise are difficulty (the value of each element is given in the code), composition and execution.

As gymnastics progresses the code of points is amended, and it is therefore the duty of the coach to have full knowledge of this code and its amendments at all times.

The purpose of the **set exercise** is to have all gymnasts performing exactly the same routine. The gymnast should follow the text, which will be available from the organising body, accurately and not add any individual movements of her own.

The **voluntary exercise** enables the gymnast to show her individual talents by making up her own routine. However, when doing this the gymnast must bear in mind the requirements of the code of points and include in her routine the appropriate difficulties, choreography, etc.

The required length of the voluntary exercise is stated in the code of points, although this may vary in local competition, when it will be the responsibility of the organising body.

Warm-up and Body Preparation

Correct warm-up and body preparation are the first steps towards becoming a first-class gymnast. Gymnasts should understand the following points:

- no training session commences without warm-up
- warm-up commences with walking, skipping, running, etc., *not* vigorous leg swinging and acrobatic skills. Gentle preparation of the body avoids accidents, and the more advanced suppling exercises must always be done when the body is thoroughly warm
- gymnastic warm-up should not be confused with warm-up for other sports. Its purpose is not just to get the gymnast warm, but to help her to learn to do movements properly, with a lot of amplitude. This means that an impression of abundance and completeness must be conveyed; all movements, whether they are acrobatic skills or dance linkages, must be carried to their furthest point.

If the warm-up is carefully planned and supervised, it can not only fully warm up the body for the session to follow, but can take care of a considerable amount of the preparatory work for the floor exercise.

It is not advisable for beginners to follow the same warm-up routine before every training session, as familiarity with the exercises leads to boredom and laziness and does not produce the desired results. As a gymnast gains experience, she will be able to perform a warm-up routine designed to her requirements. Lively music creates a happy atmosphere and helps the gymnast to extend and make full use of the exercises given to her. Changes in tempo also give the gymnast an opportunity to learn to work with music in readiness for the floor exercise.

In the early stages, a good standing position must be taught, and gymnasts must learn to achieve body tension without holding the breath. Body tension for the gymnast means a tightening of the muscles in the stomach, seat and legs. Practise relaxing and tightening your muscles until the maintenance of body tension becomes second nature. The following exercise will help the gymnast to stand well, and also to feel body tension. Stand with feet together, arms loosely by sides, head up (not tilted back), shoulders back (not hunched), and pull stomach and seat muscles in by tilting the pelvis. Raise the arms sideways and upwards to the vertical with a strong pushing action. Pushing the arms upwards, rise onto the toes, making sure that the original position of head, stomach and seat is maintained and that there is tension right through the body from the toes, pushing against the floor, to the fingertips, stretched upwards. Bring the arms down, lower the heels and maintain body tension to show a good standing position.

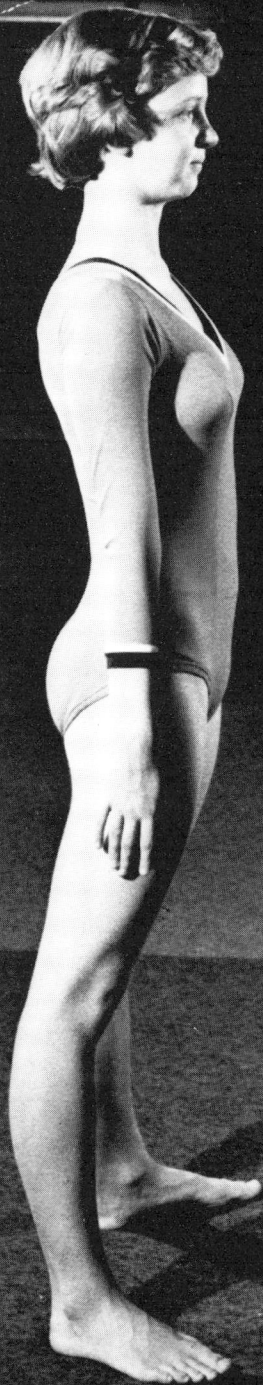

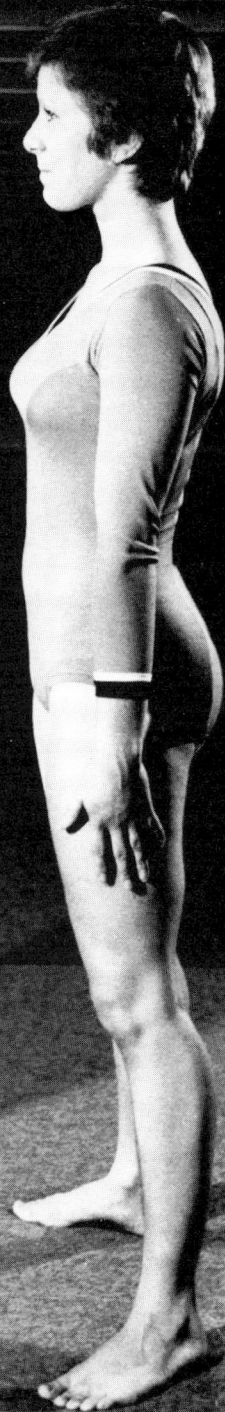

Correct standing position.
The position of the feet
will depend on the
movement to follow

Complete extension is harder to achieve in the very young gymnast, and as our champion gymnasts are becoming younger every year, coaches must pay more attention to full completion of all movements.

Suggested Warm-up

Basic exercises are given here only as a guide; they will be made much more interesting for the gymnast if they are incorporated with swinging and artistic movements. All exercises in the warm-up should be done on both sides.

- Commence with gentle running, gradually increasing speed. This will assist the run up to the vault. Do not let the arms hang loosely with no direction when running; bend the elbows and lean the shoulders slightly forward to obtain power from the run.
- Skip with a high upward spring, closing the free foot to the ankle of the supporting leg. Vary the exercise by incorporating chassé steps, gallop steps sideways, leaps and turns.
- To stretch the feet and strengthen the ankles, jump into the air, making sure that the whole of the foot is being used.
- Half and full turn jumps on two feet assist spins and twisting elements. Make sure that body

tension is maintained and that the hips and shoulders do not twist separately.

■ **Side stretching:** with feet apart and arms above the head, bend sideways to the right and the left, keeping the trunk stretched upwards. Take care not to lean the body forward.

Side stretching

■ **Leg stretching and hip suppling**: sit on the floor with both legs stretched forward and back straight (long sitting). Raise the arms sideways and upwards to the vertical and then stretch forward, reaching beyond the toes. Gently push chest onto knees, keeping head up. See facing page.
Repeat the same exercise with legs astride, arms forward, head lifted up and back flat. See above. Make sure, when you are sitting in the astride position, that the feet and knees do not roll too far inwards.

Leg stretching and hip suppling

- **Calf and thigh muscles**: sit in the 'long sitting' position with feet against a wall. Gently bounce forward so that the chest touches the knees.

- **Shoulder and hip**: standing erect with feet apart, stretch downwards to touch the ground between the feet. Bounce four times. Stand erect and circle the shoulders; become more aware of your shoulders by attempting to make the shoulder blades touch.

- **Shoulders**: clasp the hands behind the body, keeping the arms straight. Gently lift arms backwards and upwards. A partner can give assistance with this exercise.

■ **Shoulder and back:** lie on your back with knees bent, hands flat on the floor close to your head. Taking the weight onto the hands and feet, push to an arched back position, keeping shoulders and hands in line and head between arms. Pressing your heels into the floor, rock backwards and forwards, pushing the shoulders beyond the hands.

It is an advantage to incorporate splits, cartwheels and a held handstand on both legs in the warm-up. The best results are obtained if these are done to music with at least three seconds' hold on handstand and splits. A possible warm-up combination, using very little space, is described on pp. 18 and 19.

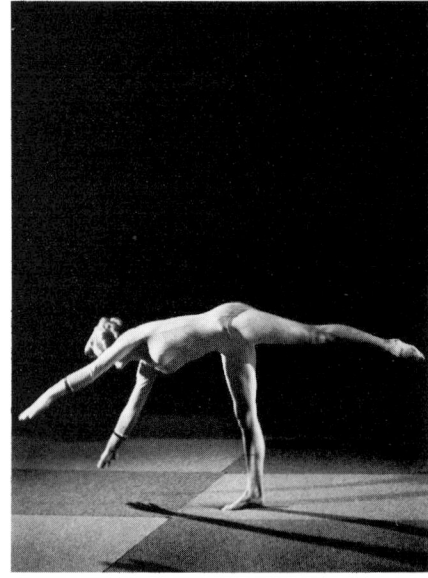

Basic link, showing the gymnast coming out of a handstand and preparing to cartwheel

Commence with the group all facing in one direction. Step forward with the right leg and kick to a handstand; hold for three seconds. Return to stand on the right leg, with the arms above the head. Make a half-turn with the weight on the toes of both feet. Step forward on the left leg and kick to a handstand; hold for three seconds. Return to stand on the left leg. Make a half-turn and repeat on both sides. When returning to stand on the left leg for the second time, make a quarter-turn to the right, with the arms held sideways. Cartwheel to the right, then to the left, and repeat on both sides. Make a quarter-turn to the left, lift the

right leg forward, bend the left knee and sit back on the floor with the arms held forward. Roll backwards to touch the floor behind your head with your feet, keeping the knees straight. Return to a sitting position, at the same time straddling the legs and making a quarter right turn into splits. Make a quarter left turn of the body and repeat the roll and splits with the left leg forward. Repeat the exercise for splits on both sides. For instructions on how to perform a handstand and cartwheel correctly, see pp. 32 and 34 respectively.

Ballet in Gymnastics

The use of ballet in gymnastics has several advantages. Simple ballet exercises assist the turn-out of the feet, knees and hips, giving a much better line to the artistic

First position

section of women's gymnastics. Ballet also strengthens the back and legs and adds poise to the arms and head.

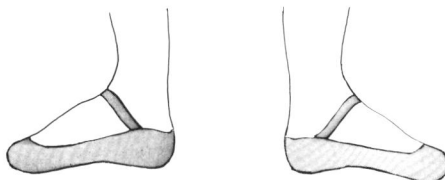

Second position

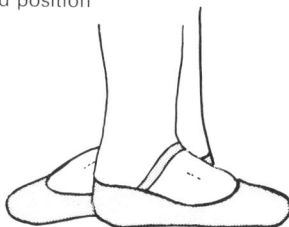

Third position

Demi Plié and Rise in First Position

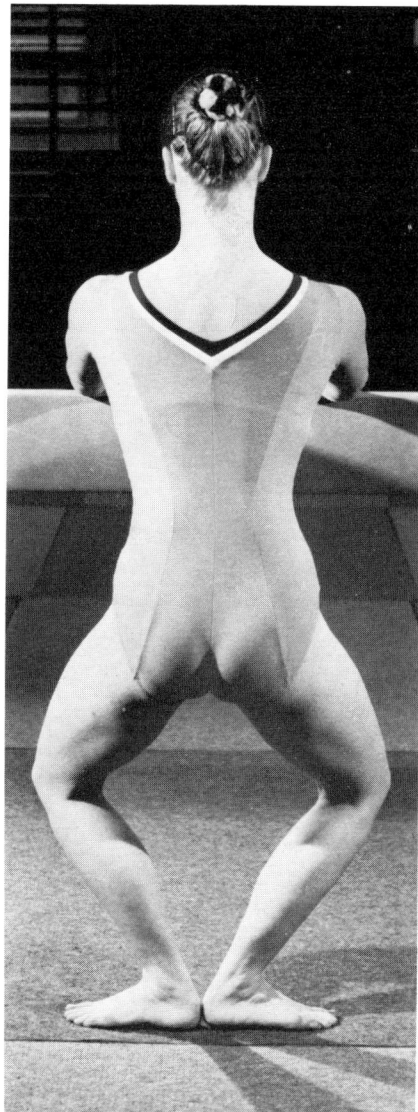

Commence facing the barre, with the hands resting lightly on the barre. The feet should be in the first position. Do a small knee bend, keeping the back straight, seat tucked in, shoulders and hips square to the barre and knees pushing out over the toes, with the weight evenly on the whole foot. Straighten the knees and rise evenly on the toes. Drop the heels and repeat. There will be a tendency when doing the knee-bend for gymnasts to have the weight on the big toe side of the foot; this is incorrect and will have the undesired affect of making the knees roll inwards.

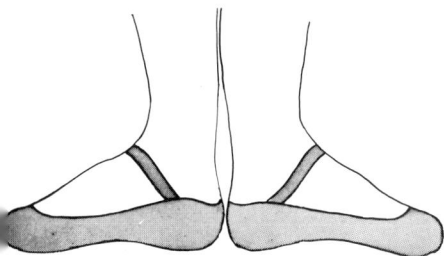

Demi plié and rise in first position

Plié in second position

Demi Plié and Rise in Second Position

This is carried out as just described, but with the feet in the second position. When the demi plié in first and second positions has been mastered correctly, the full plié in these positions may be taught.

Plié in First Position

This is performed like the demi plié but with full knees bend. The heels lift slightly just before maximum bend is reached and must be returned to the floor as early as possible whilst the knees are being straightened.

Plié in Second Position

This is performed as above, but the heels remain firmly on the floor throughout the plié.

Arm Positions

Bad head carriage and poor arm positions are common faults in young gymnasts, and the following sequence, performed to music, will help to improve the use of the head, hands and arms. Commence with feet in the first position, with the arms curving gently downwards in front of the body.

1. Lift the arms forward to shoulder height. Take the arms sideways, with the elbows leading. Allow the arms to fall gently to your sides, palms down and hands relaxed. Repeat.

2. Lift both arms forward, then lift the right arm upwards and the left arm sideways. The head follows the right arm. Bring both arms down sideways and repeat on the other side. *See the girl standing on the right of the photograph opposite.*

3. Lift both arms up to the vertical, with the arms not above the head but slightly forward. The head follows the hands. Bring both arms down sideways, with the head following the right or left hand. Repeat. *See the girl standing on the left of the photograph opposite.*

4. Lift the arms forward to shoulder height; raise the right arm upwards and drop the left arm slightly downwards. Curve both arms and tilt the head slightly to the left. Bring the arms down sideways and repeat on the other side. *See the girl kneeling in the photograph opposite.*

Maintain good posture throughout the above and make full use of the head.

Battement Tendu

Commence with the left side to the barre, the left hand resting lightly on the barre. The feet should be in the third position, with the right foot in front. Slide the right foot forwards, keeping the heel on the floor for as long as possible, until the toe is fully pointed with the knee and thigh turned out. Draw the foot back to

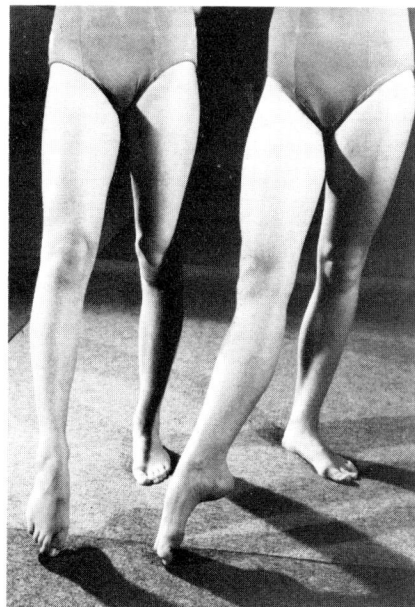

The gymnast on the right shows the correct position of the foot for ballet exercises

the starting position, returning the heel to the floor as soon as possible. Slide the foot to the right side, maintaining the turn-out of the knee and thigh so

that the heel is underneath the foot. Close the foot behind and slide backwards, again concentrating on the position of the heel. Close the foot behind, slide out to the side and close in front. Turn so that the right hand is resting on the barre and repeat on the left foot.

Note: the supporting leg should be kept straight at all times.

Grand Battement

Start as for a battement tendu, but when the foot is completely extended on the floor, lift your leg as high as possible without disturbing the position of the hips or bending the supporting leg. Rotate the leg outwardly; you should get the feeling of pushing down on the hip joint as the leg is raised. Repeat to the side and back, remembering always to slide the foot along the floor before the lift and keep the leg outwardly rotated.

Turn-out of the foot outwardly rotates the knee and thigh and if the above exercises are repeated frequently and correctly this turn-out, which is essential to the artistic side of gymnastics, will become second nature to the gymnast, who will then automatically adopt this technique throughout the floor and beam exercises.

Grand battement

An exercise to promote shoulder mobility—a partner assists the gymnast to make a full circle backwards with both arms

Suppling and Strengthening

Suppling and strengthening are an essential part of gymnastic training, particularly in the early years, as they help to develop the disciplined training programme necessary to the advanced performer.

Suppling and strengthening must never be attempted at the beginning of the session when the body is cold, but always after a good training session when the body is warm.

Suppling
Shoulders

■ Stand with your back to the barre or wall bars, hands holding the barre in a wide dislocation grip (see p. 75). Rise onto your toes and push the shoulders forward. There is often a tendency to push the stomach forward, but this is incorrect. Repeat the same exercise with the hands together on the barre.

Back

■ This exercise is performed in pairs. One gymnast lies face downwards, with her arms stretched out over her head, while the other stands behind her partner's head, takes hold of her elbows and pulls her backwards.
Repeat the exercise with the second gymnast holding her partner's knees, instead of her elbows. See right.

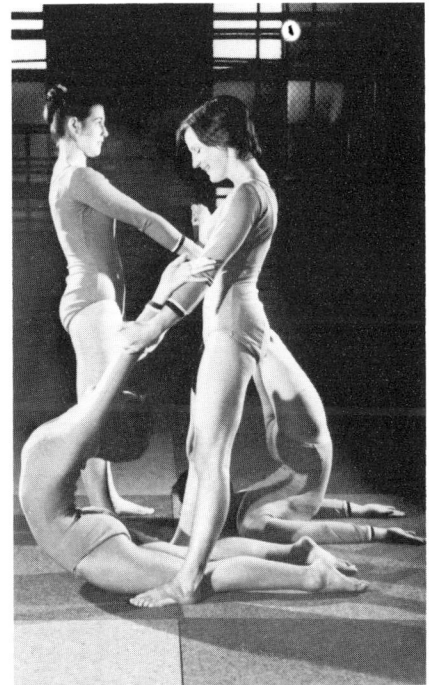

Back suppling

Back and Shoulders

■ Push up to a bridge position with your hands on another gymnast's feet. The partner then puts her hands under your shoulders and gently pulls the shoulders. Keep your arms straight. See below.

Legs

■ Stand with your back to the wall or wall bars with one leg lifted high, outwardly rotated at the hip, and the supporting leg straight, heel against the wall, toes slightly turned out. When the leg has reached maximum

height, a partner must push it very gently beyond this point. See left.

The ultimate aim is for the leg to reach splits position in all directions, but it must be coaxed gently, never forced.

Achievement of splits on the floor does not mean a gymnast can reach splits in an inverted position, i.e. walk-over, as the pressure on the floor assists the splits. Performing the splits with one foot on a bench or small beam will help to increase the leg range. See below.

Above: Leg stretching using the beam
Left: Back and shoulder supplying
Below: Extended splits

Strengthening

Back

■ Lie face downwards on a box
or horse with a partner sitting
on your feet, and your upper
body hanging over the end of
the horse. Lift and lower the
upper body, increasing the
number of lifts as strength and
stamina improve.
This exercise also helps body
tension in the upper body.

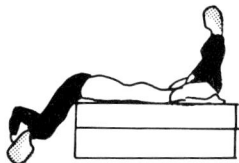

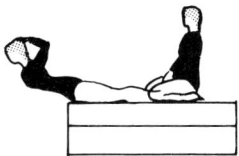

Legs

■ Sprint in a crouch position.
■ Perform squat thrusts (top
photograph).
■ Practise astride jumps across a
bench (see p. 26).

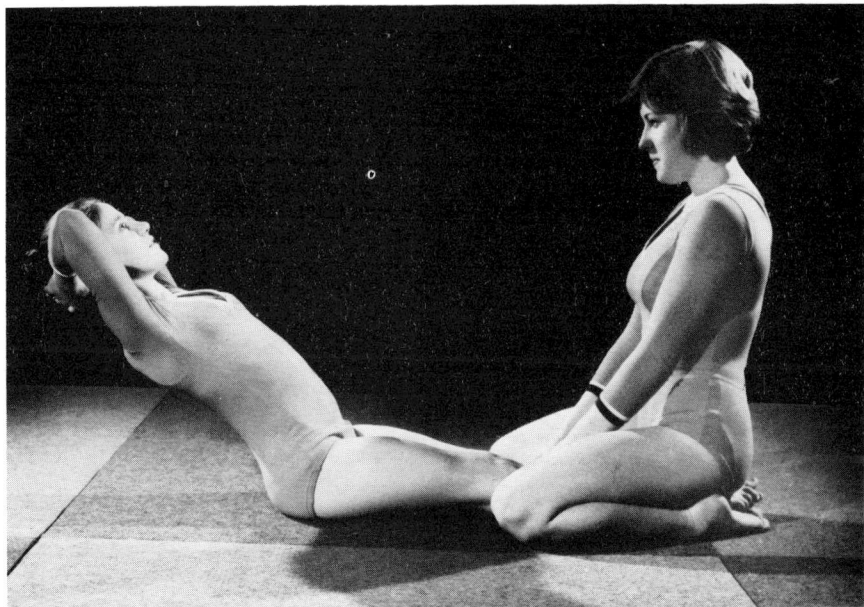

Abdomen

■ Lie on your back on the floor,
with feet hooked under a wall
bar or held by a partner. Lift up
to a sitting position; keep a
check on the number of lifts
and gradually increase it (lower
photograph).
■ Lie on your back on the floor,
holding the feet a little way off
the floor. Have a competition in
the gym to see who can hold
their feet up for the longest
time.

25

Astride jumps across a bench

■ Hang by the arms from a wall
  bar or asymmetric high bar.
  Bring the feet to the face,
  keeping a check on the number
  of repetitions, and gradually
  increasing it. A similar exercise
  can be done on the floor, as
  shown.

Arms

■ Do press-ups with the feet on a
  low wall-bar or bench.
  Increase the height of the feet
  as your strength improves.

■ Hang on a wall-bar or
  asymmetric high bar; keeping
  legs still, bend the arms until
  your head is over the bar. This
  exercise is known as 'chin-ups'.
  Running out of doors will
  increase strength and stamina and
  also provide the gymnast with a
  new interest and change of scene.
  Many suppling and strengthening
  exercises in addition to the ones
  suggested above can be beneficial
  provided they are applied with
  common sense to the individual
  needs of a particular gymnast.
  Suppling and strengthening must
  always be supervised and must
  not be carried to extremes, or
  pulled and torn muscles will occur.
  Records of the suppling and
  strengthening progression of each
  gymnast should be kept, in order
  to see whether or not there is
  improvement. If this is difficult
  with large classes, competitions
  held from time to time will
  inspire gymnasts to work harder at
  suppling and strengthening in
  order to see who can do the most
  chin-ups, squat thrusts, etc. at the
  next session.

Floor

The women's floor exercise is one of the most exciting events in sport today, with its dynamic tumbling and limitless opportunities for creativity in all types of movement and dance. The first rule of the voluntary floor exercise is that it must be designed around the individual. A sequence may be perfect for one gymnast but will not suit the personality of another.

Choice of music is equally important, as again it is not advantageous to choose a piece of music that is successful for another gymnast if it is totally unsuited to your own type of work. Unless gymnasts are fortunate enough to have a very versatile pianist who is able to work with them regularly, it is advisable to choose the music first and then compose the exercise to fit the music. The exercise must match the mood of the music throughout; if a ready-made exercise is used, the music tends to sound merely like background music. The impression the judges receive must be that every note of the music fits the exercise.

The pattern of the floor exercise should be very well thought out. It will be helpful to draw it out on a piece of paper, as this shows whether or not you have a good pattern which covers the entire floor area of 12 × 12 metres. The pattern should be as interesting and varied as possible, not a monotonous one moving from corner to corner all the time.

Floor routines should be practised in their entirety to ensure the perfect joining of the tumbling and linking movements. Combinations can be started as soon as a few skills have been learned in order that good continuity and style may prevail.

It is important for gymnasts to learn simple combinations and progress slowly to the more advanced ones, as floor exercises are so fluently linked together, with very few stops, that linkages can be very untidily done if they have not been perfected from the beginning. Extension and amplitude must be achieved from the early stages.

The average coach with a large class does not have enough time to work with each individual gymnast, and therefore much can be done for the floor exercise if basic tumbling is linked to leaps, turns, spins, etc., which can be performed with the class as a whole and which will, when needed, help the voluntary exercise to have a more finished appearance.

Young gymnasts should be given time to create their own linking movements, but they must be given plenty of ideas from the coach as to how to do this.

Linking Movements

Although the linking movements in a floor exercise are of an individual nature, a group working together can be given many ideas, as follows.

The Lunge Position

The lunge is one of the most versatile links. Although the position of the legs can only be varied by adjusting the width of the feet, the arms, upper body and head can be placed in a variety of positions. *See right and below.*

Half and Full Turns

The arms can be in any position. The legs can be bent or straight, with the knees facing forward or turned out; the supporting leg can bend.
The body can lean sideways.

Astride Sitting

The simple position of sitting astride on the floor can be reached in a variety of ways, i.e. rolls forwards, sideways or backwards, and spins. As with the lunge, the possible positions for the arms and upper body are endless.

Facing page: A basic link—roll back onto the shoulders, then roll forward through astride sitting to splits position

29

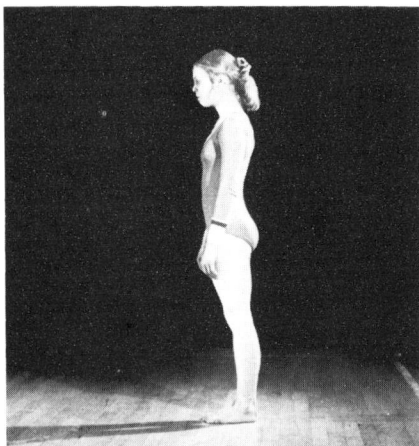

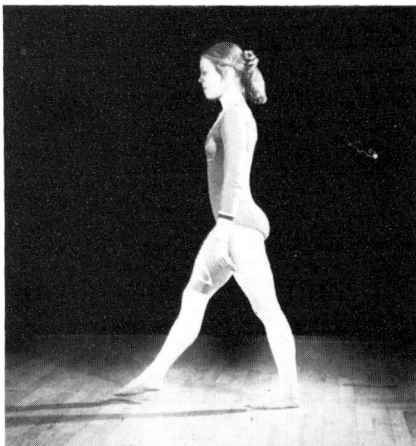

An advanced link—scissor kick holding second leg high and bending upper body backwards

Leaps and Jumps

There are endless variations of jump and leaps—here are some examples:
Sideways leap
Splits leap, stationary and forwards, with the arms in different positions
Stag leap, with one leg bent

Grand jeté, a full turn jump
Tuck jump, with the knees tucked
forward, sideways or backwards
Arched back jump, with one foot
touching the head
Half-turn, landing in an
arabesque
Taking off from two feet to land
on one.

The following combinations show the progression in skill from the beginner to the more advanced performer. You will see that the same basic elements are in both combinations, i.e. leap, turn, lunge, and astride sitting, but in the more advanced combination three leaps are joined together, the astride sitting is no longer held and the spin commences from the knee.

■ Step into a splits leap, step into a full turn on one leg. Step forward with the free leg, sit down and roll back onto the shoulders, legs held high. Roll down to an astride sitting position with the body reaching forward, using any of the arm positions. Place the right hand behind the body and cross the bent left leg over the straight right leg, at the same time making a half-turn with the body, and stand in the lunge position.

■ Make a forward splits leap and step straight into a side splits leap. Step forward with the back leg and jump with both feet together to an arched position, touching the head with the foot. Step into a high leg lift and lunge. Make a half-turn in the lunge position, sit down and roll back onto the shoulders. Come down to an astride sitting position; immediately place the right hand behind you on the floor, swing the left arm across your body to the vertical

and, pressing on the feet and right hand, raise your body off the ground, head and shoulders to the right. Return to the astride sitting position, join the legs together and sweep both legs over the right shoulder to a kneeling position. Place one foot forward on the floor and stand, at the same time performing a full spin.

Acrobatic Skills

Forward Roll

From a crouch position place the hands on the floor, with fingers

forward. Tuck the head between the arms as the hips are lifted, push from the feet and roll forward to stand. Beginners must see that the head is tucked well underneath and that the roll is felt on the shoulders, not the head.

Backward Roll

From a crouch position with the back to the mat, roll backwards in a tucked position with palms upward, so that the hands can be placed flat on the floor. When the

hands come into contact with the floor push strongly, lifting the hips to land on the floor in a crouch. The importance of the tucked position in both forward and backward rolls will be seen later in the forward and backward somersault. In these basic tumbles the gymnast is able to learn the tuck, pike, hollow, etc., which are necessary for more advanced gymnastics, and it is important for the mind to become familiar with these shapes early in training.

Handstand

Place the hands on the floor, shoulder-width apart and fingers forward, and kick to an inverted position. The back and arms should be straight, with the head coming naturally in line with the body. Very young beginners should be well supported for the handstand, as neither the arms nor the legs are sufficiently strong to complete the movement without assistance. Learn the handstand on a mat until you have achieved balance and learned the correct way of returning to stand, which is by splitting the legs and landing on one foot. Gymnasts must not

Backward roll to handstand

get into the habit of holding the handstand with a hollow back, though in some cases they may find it easier. It is wrong and will be very hard to correct. Constant practice in the correct position is the way to a perfect handstand. Gripping the floor with the fingers will assist in controlling the balance.

Progress from the handstand to the handstand forward roll, and backward roll to handstand (see above).

Cartwheel

This movement is performed sideways, and as the name suggests is a complete inverted sideways wheel of the body to an even rhythm count of four; i.e. for a left-handed cartwheel the count is left hand 1, right hand 2, right foot 3, left foot 4. Beginners may find it difficult to wheel sideways and transfer the weight from one arm to the other and coaches will find forms and box horses a valuable aid to learning this sideways movement.

The cartwheel must always be learned to both left and right. Progress from the cartwheel to a dive cartwheel, one-arm cartwheel, cartwheel to handstand, and cartwheel to splits.

Handstand to Bridge

Before progressing to the handstand to bridge, gymnasts must learn the bridge position. Lie on your back with knees bent and heels close to seat, hands flat on the floor close to your ears. Lifting the hips upwards, push strongly from hands and feet until arms and legs are straight and you have reached a fully arched bridge position. Progress from this to a momentary handstand and allow the feet to reach over to the floor in the bridge position, keeping your shoulders over your hands. This movement should be controlled and you must be able to hold a firm bridge position without collapse before learning to stand. To stand, push from the hands immediately the feet arrive on the floor, keeping the legs straight, lifting the hips high and bringing the arms over the head. Note that the heels are flat on the floor in the bridge position.

Progression from a forward walk-over to a walk-over using one arm only

Forward Walk-over

Commence as for the handstand but allow the leading leg to continue over the head to the floor, the legs passing through the splits position. Press the leading foot firmly into the floor with the heel flat and lift the hips forwards and upwards, pushing from the hands to bring the upper body quickly to the vertical. Hold the second leg high as the body is lifted, so that you are ready to walk-out into the next movement.

Progression from the backward walk-over. Note the position of the hips in the top right-hand photograph, allowing the leg to cut through the arm to the splits position

a

b

c

g

h

i

d

e

f

Backward Walk-over

Stand with your weight on one leg, the other stretched forward, toe pointed, and arms overhead. Keeping the head between the arms, bend the body backwards to bring the hands to the floor, simultaneously lifting the forward leg over the head and passing through the splits position to land on one leg. Push from the floor quickly with your hands to arrive in a standing position. The weight will now be on the forward leg, the other leg being stretched backwards in preparation for placing on the floor for a second walk-over or the next movement.

Handspring

(see sequence above)

The handspring is a fast
handstand, the speed of the legs
together with the thrust through
the shoulders and push from the
hands giving it the forward and
upward momentum necessary for
the gymnast to land on her feet. It
is often wrongly interpreted in
the learning stages as a quick
handstand to bridge and stand, but
in fact there is no back arch in the
handspring.

The gymnast should first learn to
perform a handstand with the legs
joining together quickly. To do
this you must thrust strongly with
the leading leg as the rear leg
kicks backwards, and the leading
leg must then join the rear leg
before the handstand position is
reached. This can be practised
with a partner, first from a
standing position and then with
one or two preparatory steps, the
last one of which is a small hop on
one leg. The leading leg and the

arms reach forward with the foot
thrusting strongly from the floor as
the rear leg kicks backwards to the
handstand. Keep the body tight.
Coaches can assist the gymnast to
feel the push from the hands and
extension through the shoulders

by supporting the fast handstand
at the hips and lifting the gymnast
in an upward direction so that the
hands are off the floor. *See the
two photographs below.*
Support can be given at the
shoulder and back to give the

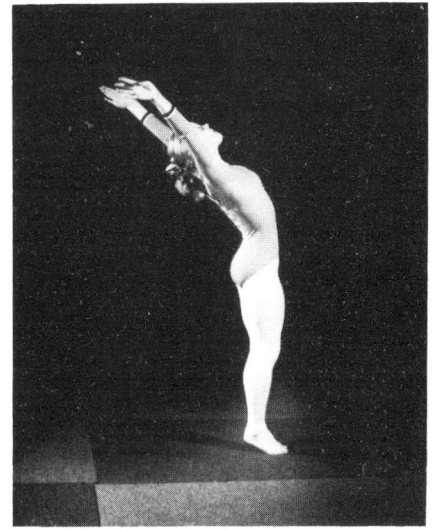

handspring lift. To assist in giving the feeling of flight in the handspring, as this is often the most difficult part, use a springboard. The hands are placed at the top of the board and the landing is on to the floor.

Progress from the ordinary handspring to a handspring landing on one leg, which is a very useful linking movement for the floor exercise. However, as it is a very common fault to perform this movement as a fast forward walk-over without any thrust from the hands or body tension in the handstand, it is necessary to learn the handspring to two feet first.

Back Flip

Stand with feet together. Bend the knees and lean backwards, shoulders in line with hips, arms forward. As the body loses balance swing the arms upward, push the hips forward and drive strongly from the feet, heels down, to rotate backwards, passing through a momentary handstand. Push from the hands and snap both legs down together to stand.

Round-off or Arab Spring

A good round-off is a necessity as it precedes most of the fast tumbling runs in the floor exercise.

The round-off commences in a similar manner to the fast cartwheel, but the legs are brought together in the vertical position and the body makes a quarter-turn inwards so that the gymnast lands facing the direction of the approach run.

As in the handspring, the legs must be fast with a strong thrusting action from the leading leg to pass through vertical. There must be a strong push from the hands to land on the feet with the arms coming upwards in preparation for a half turn or back flip. If there is no pushing action from the hands to the feet, the round-off will not have the necessary speed and lift to connect with the next movement.

Tucked Backward Somersault

Coaches should see that gymnasts learn the standing backward somersault before progressing to the round-off backward somersault or the round-off back flip backward somersault. That way, the gymnast will be fully aware of the body position at all times.

From a standing position, swing the arms upward and jump into the air, keeping the body tight. At the height of the jump bring the arms down, pull the knees up to the chest and rotate backwards in the tucked position. When the body has turned over, extend the arms and legs to land.

Backward Somersault— Hollow

The difference between this and the tucked somersault is the body position, which is arched throughout the backward somersault. The same upward jump is required but the arms remain upward while the body rotates backwards; the head is held back, chest and hips are lifted upward to maintain the hollow position, and the legs are kept straight.

Round-off back flip tucked backward somersault, followed by an immediate jump from two feet into a lunge position

Free cartwheel—note the strong push from the feet and the speed at which the leading leg rises on take-off

Free Cartwheel

A good fast cartwheel with a strong thrusting action from the leading leg should be mastered before the free cartwheel is attempted. Learn the free cartwheel from one step with assistance at the hips. There should be a strong thrusting action from the leading leg, which pushes hard against the floor whilst the back leg lifts quickly in an upward direction to be followed by the thrusting leg. The legs must lift quickly and be directed upwards in order that the body weight does not drop. While a gymnast is learning the free cartwheel, a spring-board will assist in giving height to the movement.

Supporting the free cartwheel in the hips will allow the young gymnast to feel the movement and see the necessity of using the leading foot and speeding up the leg action

Free Walk-over

Commence as for the free cartwheel, with a strong push from the floor and upward thrust with the legs. Swing the arms downward and backward to assist the lift upward, and keep the back arched in the shape of the walk-over.

Again, a springboard can be of assistance in the learning stages.

Forward Somersault

The use of a springboard is invaluable for this somersault. As in the backward somersault, a high upward jump at the beginning is necessary, with the arms reaching forward and upward. At the height of the jump pull the arms down, tuck the knees up and rotate forward. When the body has turned over, extend the arms and legs to land.

Beam

Complete mastery of the balance beam should begin from the first moment you step on to it. It has proved a disaster for many competitors and must therefore be tackled with persistence and dedication, however boring this may be. A gymnast must be prepared, in the early stages of her training, to spend a great deal of time on basic beamwork. Body tension is a 'must' on the beam, along with an ability to think and move in a straight line.

Beamwork is performed on a straight plank of wood 10 cm (4 in.) wide, and as a result of this, most movements must be performed with shoulders and hips square to the beam. Slack and twisted bodies will give uneven distribution of weight and result in a fall. All turns must be fully completed with hips and shoulders moving together. A twist of the hips independent of the shoulders or vice versa will again result in overbalancing. Legs and arms must be able to move independently, e.g. high leg lifts

and expansive arm and upper body movements must not throw the body off balance and allow the body tension to collapse.

If your training time is limited and in addition to the regular beam or beams you have training beams and benches, coaches may find it beneficial to warm up on the beams instead of the floor. Many of the floor exercises can be adapted to the beam and music assists flow of movement and gives confidence to the gymnast who has difficulty expressing artistic ability on the beam. A line of two or three benches (if necessary place mats on the top for confidence) gives a good situation for linking agilities. Five or six backward walk-overs at a good speed instil confidence for two backward walk-overs on the high beam.

Apply the 'think and move straight' policy to agilities, as a roll or walk-over with twisted hips or shoulders will not be successful. To prevent twisting, the gymnast should look straight down the line

of the beam before commencing forward movements so that she will retain a mental picture of the line and width of the beam after she has started to roll, etc. Simple linkages should be taught from the beginning, and as ability increases many repetitions of set and voluntary exercises should be performed with increased repetitions on the weaker parts. New gymnasts should try and establish a discipline from the beginning for attacking the whole of the exercise, particularly the parts they do not perform very well.

Introduction to beamwork should always be by bench or training beam, the coach deciding when a gymnast is proficient enough to graduate to the higher beam. Walking on a high beam can be a daunting experience to a young gymnast who has never been on a beam and much better results are obtained if the beginner is at least confident of walking on a width of 10 cm (4 in.).

Beam for Beginners

Stand at the end of the beam with one foot pointed forward, arms out sideways, head erect, shoulders relaxed (not hunched), stomach pulled in, and back straight, not hollow.

Coaches should insist on the gymnast commencing her beam exercise correctly from the very beginning, as this will give her the composure she needs later on for much more difficult exercises. In preparation for the advanced beam exercise, young gymnasts should not scramble up onto the beam and start walking without first gaining composure.

Walk briskly along the beam putting the toes down first, with hips and shoulders in a straight line at right angles to the beam. On reaching the end of the beam, place the feet together and jump to the ground, paying attention to the jump as this constitutes good landing practice.

Repeat this procedure substituting running, step hops and chassé steps. Walk two or three steps, close the feet together, bend the knees to crouch with arms down by sides and rise onto the toes, lifting arms sideways. Repeat to the end of the beam.

Four or five gymnasts stand on their toes together on the beam, right foot in front, feet slightly apart and arms by sides. Make a half-turn to the left, without

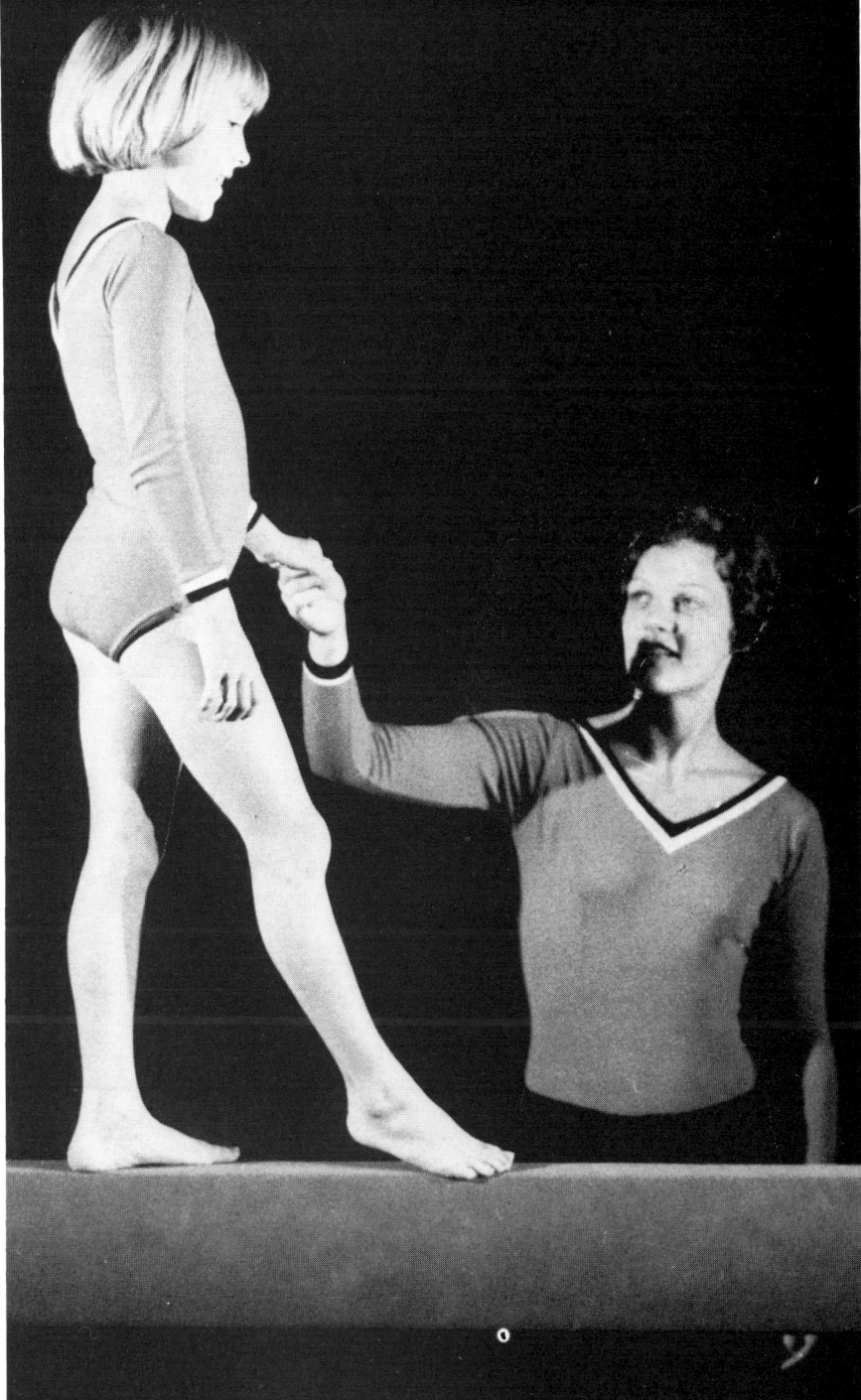

straight, depending on the ability
of the gymnast). Step forward on
the left foot, keeping the right leg
bent behind. Walk forward one
step and repeat on the opposite
side. During both movements, use
any swinging or circling arm

using the arms. Repeat to the
right.

From the basic half-turn move to a
half-turn on one leg, knee
outwardly rotated, free foot on
calf. Use the arms above the head
on the turn, but make sure this
arm movement does not throw
your body off balance. Turn both
ways.

Step forward on the right leg and
lift the left leg horizontally
forward (the knee may be bent or

Learning body
control when the
weight is taken on
one leg

movements; this will give the gymnast confidence in standing on one leg in preparation for arabesques, etc.

Stand with the right foot in front of the left, then rise onto your toes. With a slight flexing of the knees, spring upward, landing in the same position on the beam, knees slightly bent. After performing a few repetitions, change feet so that the left foot is in front. Eventually change feet in the air, e.g. take off with the right foot in front and land with the left foot in front. The height of the spring will improve as confidence is gained.

Two or three gymnasts may work together on the beam on this exercise, which is a basic mount to familiarise new gymnasts with gripping and lying on the beam. Place both hands on the beam and jump to the front support position. Circle one leg backwards over the beam to sit astride the beam. Place the hands behind the body and lift both legs onto the beam. Lie down, gripping the beam behind your head (see the photograph above right). Bring the legs over to touch the beam behind your head; the legs must pass over the beam in a straight line. Return to a sitting position, both legs on one side of the beam. Place one hand forward on the beam, swing the legs back and push from your hand to land on the floor.

Progressive Beam-work: Mounts
Single Leg Squat

With a short run, place both hands on the beam, spring from two feet and squat with one leg between the hands, to arrive in a forward astride sitting position on the beam with arms straight and head erect.

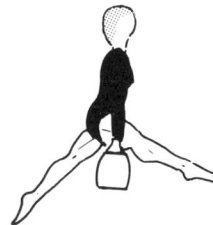

Two-legged Squat

With a short run, place both hands on the beam and, springing from both feet, squat both legs bent onto the beam, feet between hands. The shoulders should be over the beam during the squat. The two-legged squat can be carried a stage further by squatting both legs between the hands over the beam to a sitting position.

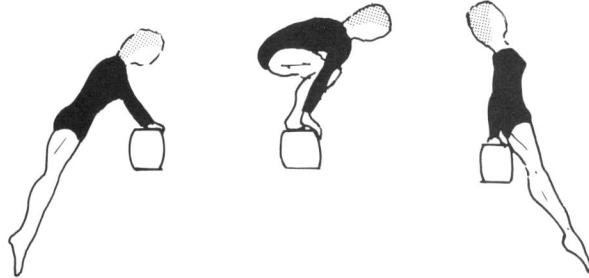

Straddle

Placing the hands on the beam, spring from both feet, lifting the hips high. Place the feet on either side of the hands, shoulders forward and legs straight.

Straddle Over

Commence as for the straddle mount, but the gymnast must have sufficient strength and control to hold the weight of her body whilst the legs are being carried over the beam. Holding the weight in this straddle position should first be practised on the beam or asymmetric bar.

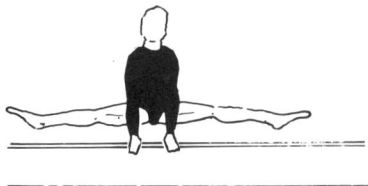

Step-on Mount

Commence with your right side to the beam; from an oblique angle, run and take off from the left foot, right hand on the beam. Place first the right foot then the left foot on the beam and land in a crouch position, keeping the body weight over the right leg. Remove the right hand from the beam immediately on arrival of the right foot. This could be performed on either leg.

Take-off may also be from the right foot with the left side of body to the beam, as shown. Progressions; this mount may be performed without the use of the hands either to a crouch or to a

standing position. Swing the arms forward and upward on take-off, keeping the body weight forward. It may also be performed from the end of the beam to crouch, to stand or to arabesque.

Forward Roll

Stand facing the end of the beam. With a run, place both hands on top of the beam; jump, hips high, and forward roll onto your feet. If the hips are not lifted high over the head, there will be a tendency to land with the top of the head instead of the neck on the beam.

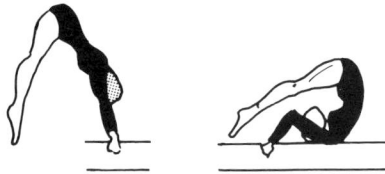

Fencing

Approach from an oblique angle with right side to the beam. Place the right hand on the beam and, taking off from the left foot, throw the right leg, closely followed by the left, up and over the beam to land sitting on the beam with both legs over to the right side. Take-off may be from the other side. Progression: may be performed without hands, keeping the weight forward as in the step-on mount.

Handstand

Facing the end of the beam, run, placing both hands on top of the beam, and jump with straight arms to an inverted pike position, legs straddled. When the hips are over the shoulders, join the legs together in a handstand and either forward roll or walk-over.

Forward Roll

The roll should be fast to eliminate loss of balance. The back should be rounded, as on the floor, to enable the shoulders to lift off the beam immediately, and the arms should reach forward to maintain balance. Starting and finishing positions of the roll may be varied when a good roll has been achieved, but for beginners, rolling from crouch to crouch is the most satisfactory method. It is easier to roll quickly from a crouch position on two feet, and bringing the two feet in quickly to crouch at the end of the roll with the arms reaching forward lifts the seat off the beam.

Progressive Beam-work: Acrobatic Skills

Although most of the acrobatic skills to be performed on the beam will have been learnt on the floor, transfer to the beam should not be made until the skills have been performed correctly and confidently on a straight line first on the floor and then on a low beam. In this way excess supporting by the coach can be eliminated and you will see a much more confident gymnast in the competitive situation.
The following skills are all performed with the hands on top of the beam.

Forward roll from crouch

Forward roll from lunge

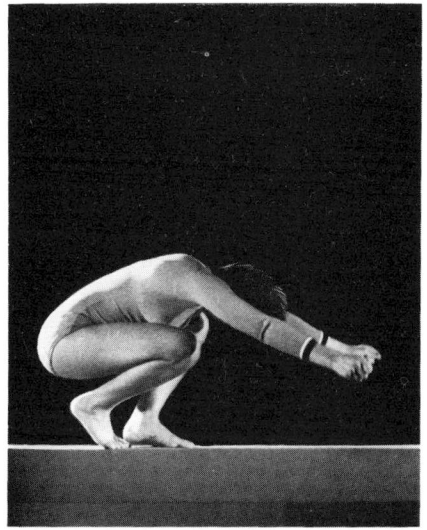

Backward Roll

As in the forward roll, there must be continuity. The gymnast should not at any time be lying flat on the beam. The back must be rounded and the legs lifting overhead before the hands touch the beam.

Backward roll to crouch

Backward roll to arabesque

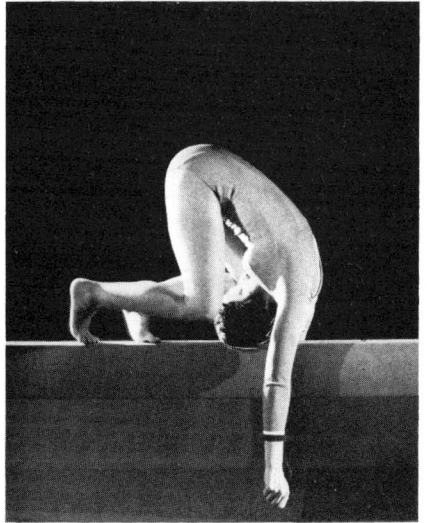

Start the roll from sitting, standing or crouch, to finish kneeling on one knee, in a crouch, on one or two feet or sitting astride the beam. Beginners should start by sitting on the beam and roll to finish with one knee or one foot in a crouch.

Free Forward Roll

Commence in a crouch position, arms overhead. Lifting the hips and pushing from the feet, reach the arms forward and downward, head tucked underneath and back rounded. The shoulders come into contact with the beam as the feet leave the beam.

Handstand

A handstand along the beam is more difficult than a handstand on the floor, due to the position of the hands and shoulders. It can only be truly mastered by practising on the beam width of 10 cm (4 in.). The handstand can either be straight with the legs together or in a split with one leg bent (stag).

For the handstand along the beam, the hands are placed with the thumbs on top and the fingers down the side.

A handstand sideways on the beam can be likened to the handstand on the floor as the arms are shoulder-width apart and the fingers can grip the beam to maintain balance. This handstand is usually reached from the side by a half-cartwheel to handstand.

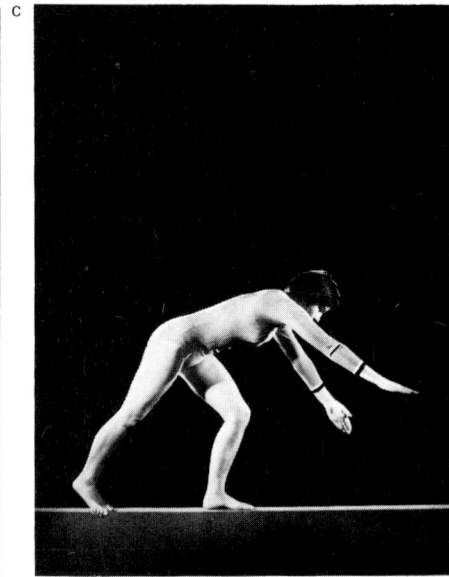

One-arm cartwheel performed on the second arm

Cartwheel

The cartwheel is performed with alternating hands, as on the floor, but the movement will be much shorter due to the first leg landing closer to the hands. The hands must be lifted from the beam and the body raised immediately the foot lands on the beam. The cartwheel can be done completely sideways or with an inward turn. For beginners the inward turn gives a firmer landing base for the feet. Progression: one-arm cartwheel performed on the second arm. Cartwheel inward turn to handstand along the beam: start as for a cartwheel then, moving the first hand alongside the second hand, turn inwards into a handstand (see diagram).

e

f

g

h

a   b   c

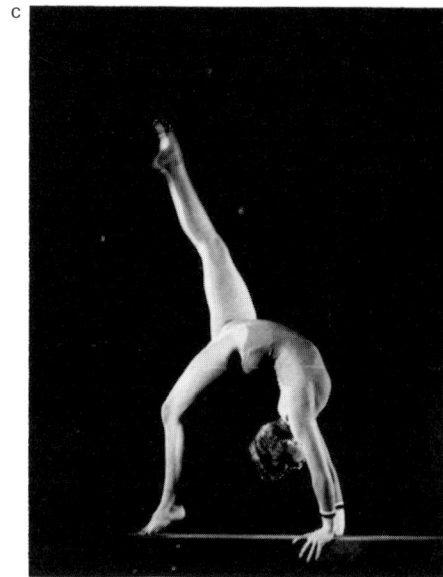

Backward Walk-over

Commence with arms vertical,
head between arms, one foot
stretched forward, and tension in
the body and legs. Arms and head
bend backwards together as the
initial leg lifts; pass through a
backward handstand with split
legs to place your foot on the
beam and immediately lift the
body to stand with arms overhead.

Progress to the backward walk-over to
handstand, straddling the legs to finish
sitting astride the beam

d

e

f

g

h

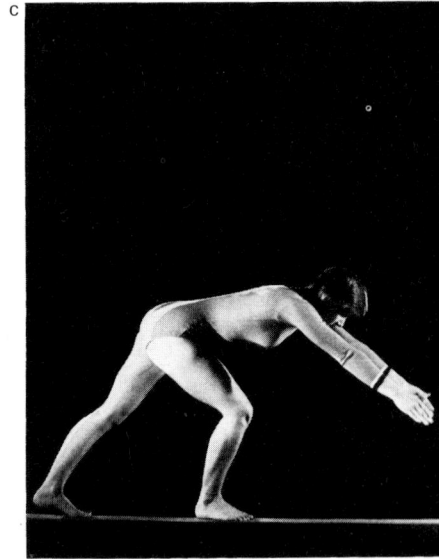

Forward Walk-over

The walk-over on the beam
requires a supple back and
shoulders and great care must be
taken to see that the walk-over is
straight before being transferred
from the floor to the beam. As the
base of the hands is narrowed on
the beam, so is the path of the
legs.

The legs must walk straight over
the base of the hands and not, as
is often the tendency, move round
to one side causing loss of
balance.

Also, to enable the upper body to
rise quickly to a standing position,
the foot which lands on the beam
must be closer to the hands. The
head must not be left behind on
the rise to stand.

a   b   c

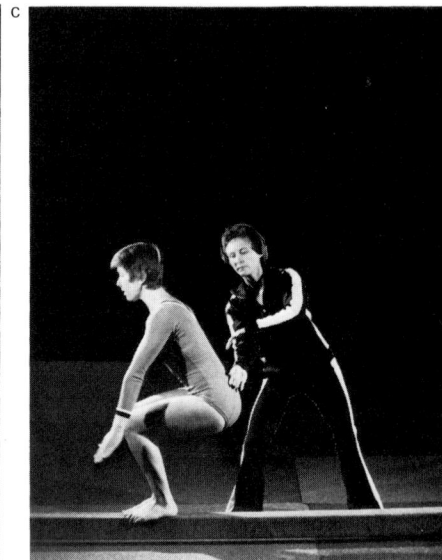

Note the arm position of the coach. When the gymnast commences the backward throw the arm is moved under her back to grip the waist, the second arm of the coach moving instantly to the waist on the near side

Back Flip

Perform a back flip on a floor line, getting the feel of moving backwards at speed with hands together, bearing in mind that the back flip on the beam will not travel backwards to the same extent as the back flip on the floor, and will therefore be higher. Progress to a floor beam but have plenty of mats and an experienced person to support, as the first attempt on a narrow beam often results in bent arms or missing the beam altogether.

The back flip must not be transferred to a higher beam until it is performed with certainty and without support. Then the progression should be by gradual heightening of the beam and the constant attendance of a coach.

e

f

h

i

Static Linking Balances

It is necessary to include in the beam exercise a variation of static balances. These are usually an extension of a movement, i.e. backward walk-over step back into lunge. Static balances are held momentarily and must not break the continuity of the exercise.

Two variations of the static balance

Travelling and Turning along the Beam

Leaps, jumps, spins, etc. breathe life into the beam exercise. An exercise composed of acrobatic skills and static balances only will be very dull and monotonous. From the beginning the gymnast must practise stationary and travelling jumps on the beam so that these can be incorporated at a more advanced level with variations of leaps, spins, turns, chassé steps and high leg lifts. The 360° spin can be done with the free leg and arms in any position. The spin should be performed quickly to avoid loss of balance, with the weight controlled over the supporting leg, shoulders and hips in line, and body tense.

Dismounts

As the finale to the exercise, the dismount must be practised constantly so that a well-executed landing is performed every time. Land on the toes, then push the heels down, knees slightly bent. When the body is in complete control straighten the knees and extend the body upwards.

Splits leap along the beam ▶

Round-off Dimount

Standing at the end of the beam,
commence as for a cartwheel but
join the legs together as in the
handstand and make a quarter turn
inwards. Push with the hands
when the feet have passed the
inverted position to land with feet
together, facing the end of the
beam.

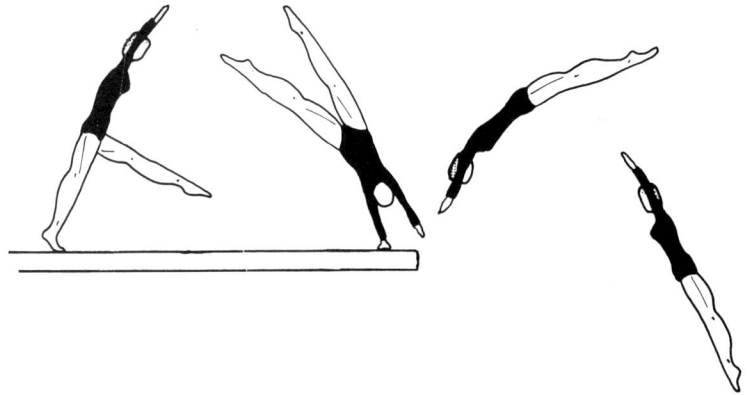

Round-off dismount

Handspring dismount

Cartwheel

This is performed as a cartwheel
on the beam, but the legs join
together as the second hand is
placed and the body wheels
sideways, pushing away from the
beam with the second hand.
A common fault when learning
this dismount for the first time is
failure to join the legs together
before landing.

Handspring

Facing the end of the beam, take
one or two steps, place the hands
on the end of the beam and kick to
a handstand, joining legs together
quickly. Push with the hands to
land with your back to the beam.
The body must maintain a straight
position throughout the dismount
—there must be no back arch. The
feet reach forward on landing to
avoid over-rotation.
To assist the gymnast to feel her
body position, have a supporter on
either side of the beam. As the
gymnast kicks to the handstand,
hold her arm and seat and lift her
in a straight body position away
from the beam to land. See
opposite.

Handstand Quarter Turn

Commence as for cartwheel to side handstand. On reaching the handstand, take the body weight on one arm and lift the other arm off the beam sideways, at the same time turning the body towards the supporting arm. Keep the head and chest well up and the body will stay hollow until landing. If there is insufficient arm and head lift, the body will pike to land.

Free Dismounts

Free Cartwheel and Free Walk-over

These free dismounts are performed as on the floor, except that the legs are joined together in the inverted position in preparation for landing. There should be a good strong push from the foot on take-off and the skill must be performed at waist height so that the gymnast has plenty of time to complete the movement and prepare for landing.

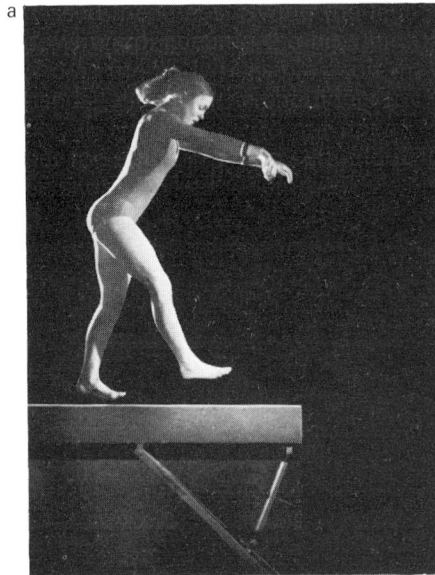

Free cartwheel off the end of the beam

Forward and Backward Somersaults (Tucked)

These two movements are performed in the initial stages from two feet, as on the floor.
A popular progression of the backward somersault is the addition of the cartwheel to land at the end of the beam and an immediate tucked, piked or hollow backward somersault. At a more advanced level, the twisting backward somersault can be used. All free dismounts from the beam progress by changing the shape, i.e. pike, hollow, etc., or by adding a twisting movement, but it is essential that all gymnasts perform the basic movement correctly and competently before progressing to these more advanced skills.

c   d   e

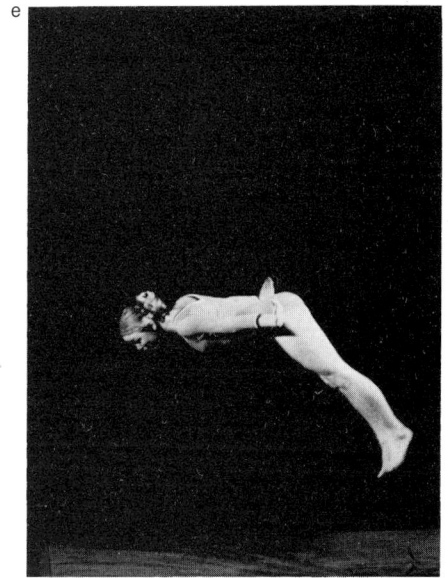

Piked free walk-over off the end of the beam

b   c

Asymmetric Bars

The necessity for perfection in basic training applies very strongly to this piece of apparatus. Basic elements must be taken to their utmost point from the very beginning so that this becomes second nature to the gymnast, giving her freedom to concentrate later on more advanced skills. The asymmetric bars exercise consists predominantly of swinging elements, moving from one bar to the other continuously. It is therefore important for the young gymnast to link elements together from the beginning to obtain this feeling of continuity. Exercises should be given for developing strength in the arms, shoulders and abdominal region. Extreme suppleness is also required in the hips to enable gymnasts to move quickly in and out of a pike position.

Young gymnasts should be encouraged to wear handguards. If the handguards are worn in the early stages for basic elements, then the gymnast will become familiar with them and problems will not arise at a later stage when they are a necessity, because of concentrated training.

Positions on the Bar

Facing low bar

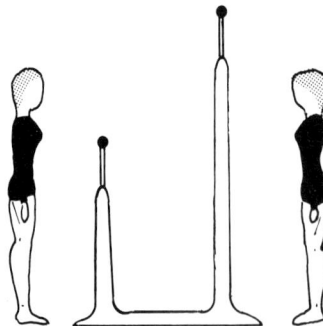

Facing high bar

Front support

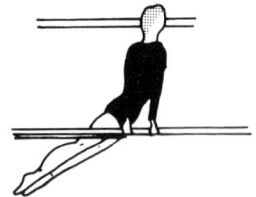

Back support

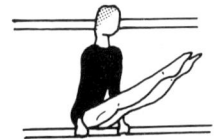

Front lying position

Back lying position

Long hang
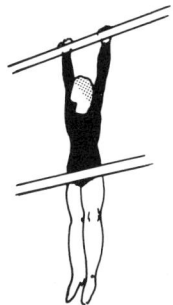

Mill support

Half inverted hang

Mixed
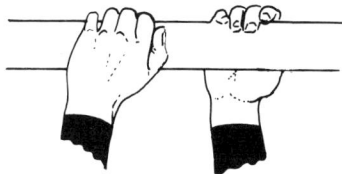

Dislocation

Handguard
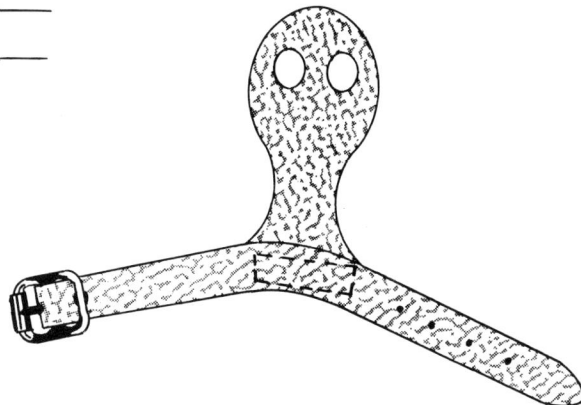

Grips

Regular
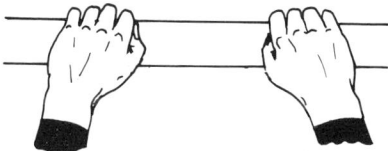

Reverse
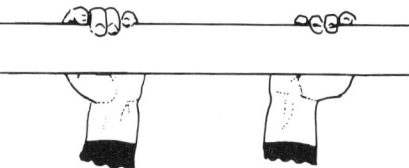

Mounts

A springboard may be used for mounts.

Jump to Front Support

Stand facing the low bar, with hands in a regular grip shoulder-width apart. Jump from two feet to front support. A good strong push from the feet is needed, with the arms pushing down on the bar to straighten the elbows.

If this start is performed with a springboard and a few running steps a lay-out will be possible before coming to front support. From the front support position, swing the legs forward slightly, swing backwards and lift away from the bar to a horizontal position, keeping the shoulders over the bar. Keep the body tight and straight and aim to go above the horizontal.

Long Underswing and Upstart

Jump backwards into a piked hang, hands in a regular grip on the low bar. The head should be between the arms. Allow the body to swing forward, feet close to the floor, until the pike unfolds and full extension is reached. At the end of the swing pike the body sharply, bringing the toes back towards the bar. The speed of the legs is important at this point; if

Backward Hip Circle from Two Feet

Stand with the hands on the low bar in a regular grip. Jump upwards from two feet; bring the hips in to the bar, allow the shoulders to drop back and backward circle. The body should be only slightly bent during the circle.

the legs are slow the hips will drop low underneath the bar and swing and timing will be lost. Keep the legs moving in an upward direction until the bar has passed the knees. Swing the legs downward, keeping the hips high, and as the body rises press on the hands, allowing the shoulders to rise above the bar. Do not open out too soon; the body should still be slightly piked when the

upstart is nearly completed, enabling the shoulders, arms and hips to be in a good position over the bar to allow the legs to swing backwards away from the bar. At this point the arms may bend slightly to cope with the push into the lay-out. The upstart does not finish in front support but continues into a lay-out in preparation for the next movement.

Long underswing and upstart

Long Underswing Squat, Both Legs through to Upstart

Perform a long underswing, as for the long underswing and upstart. At the end of the swing the body pikes sharply and remains in a pike position as the feet pass between the hands and over the top of the low bar, the body rising through a 'V' sit position to finish sitting on the bar.

Long underswing squat, both legs through to upstart. The rise to sitting on the bar must be in a piked position, as shown on the right, not a hollow position, as shown on the left

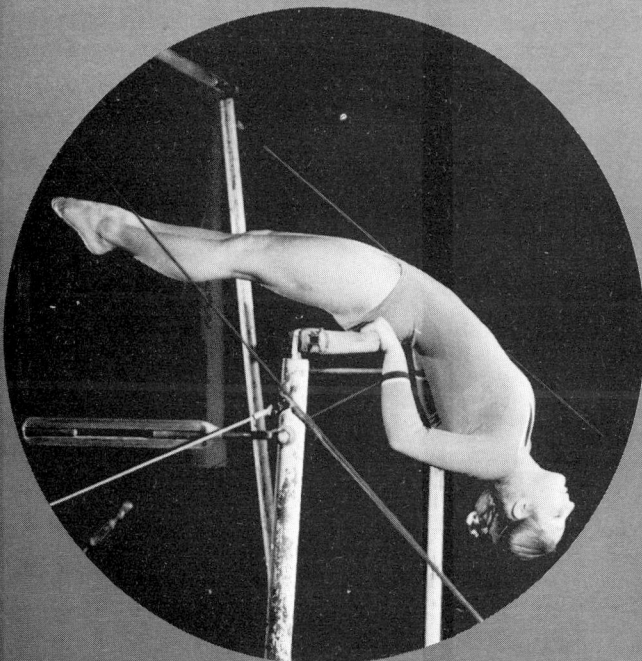

Squat and straddle mounts

Squat and Straddle Mounts

These are vault-type mounts using a springboard which can be practised in the first instance to land on the low bar in either squat or straddle. As the gymnast progresses, the squat or straddle can be taken over the low bar to catch the high bar, giving more continuity to the mount. See above.

The springboard should not be too near the bar as sufficient flight and a good strong push from the hands are necessary to overcome the height of the bar.

Circling Movements
Backward Hip Circle

This is a basic movement which, together with the upstart, plays an important part in the most advanced bar routines and must therefore be practised constantly. From front support with the hands in a regular grip, swing the legs slightly forward in preparation for the lay-out, then swing the legs backwards to a horizontal position, keeping the shoulders over the bar and the body straight. On the return swing bring the hips in to the bar, drop the shoulders back, keeping the head in line, and circle backwards round the bar to front support, holding the legs behind in preparation for the next movement.

Forward Hip Circle

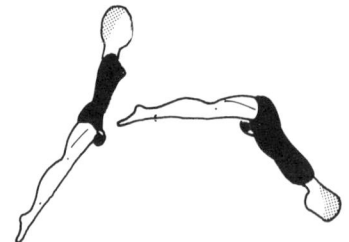

Start in a front support, with the hands in a regular grip. Lift high so that the bar is held against the top of the legs, with body extended and head up. Fall forward with a slightly hollow back until head and shoulders have passed the horizontal, and pike the body sharply so that the head is moving towards the knees. Keeping the

Forward hip circle

Backward hip circle

bar in the hip joint, swing the legs backwards under the bar to a front rest. The wrists should drop under the bar at the start of the movement in preparation for the last stage, when the hands are needed on top of the bar. Timing is essential in the forward circle. Do not rush the fall forward; move the hands before swinging the legs backwards, then the bar will remain in the hip joint and the movement will be successful.

Single-leg Uprise

Sit astride the bar with the hands in a regular grip. Take the weight on the hands and move the seat upwards and backwards, allowing the body to swing under the bar. The hips should be allowed to swing to the fullest extent so as not to interfere with the timing of the movement, and the legs should be kept fairly close

Free forward hip circle to catch the high bar

together without touching the bar. If the back leg drops away from the bar it will prevent a good extended swing. On the return swing, to rise above the bar keep the forward leg close to the body and shoot through and over the bar, allowing the leg to connect with the bar at the top of the thigh. In the early stages of this movement there will be a tendency to attempt the rise above with hollow back and bent knee, but this will be corrected as soon as the gymnast is familiar with the dropping back movement.

Two-leg Uprise

Start in a back support position, with the hands in a regular grip. Lift the body to a pike position clear of the bar and swing backwards underneath the bar. At the end of the swing return to the back support position, keeping the body piked and pressing downwards with the hands and backs of thighs. Do not allow the legs to drop below sitting position on the bar until the head and shoulders have risen above.

The piked position used at the start of the backward seat circle and the two-legged uprise

Backward Seat Circle

Start in the back support position with the hands in a regular grip. Lift the body to a pike position clear of the bar, hips slightly in front of the hands. The body then drops backwards, shoulders leading, to completely circle the bar, finishing in an open back support position. Keep the hips close to the bar whilst circling and do not open out to the back support until body weight and hips are above the bar. The movement of the wrists from underneath to the top of the bar on the second part of the movement must be quick.

Forward Seat Circle

This is a complete circle of the bar in a pike position, with the hands in reverse grip. Taking the weight on the hands, lift the body clear of the bar with hips high behind the hands and head forward. Fall forward, reaching away from the bar; do not drop suddenly underneath the bar, as this will give no impetus to the rise above it. The hands move round the bar with arms straight to allow the gymnast to return to a piked sitting position on the bar.

Straddle Half-sole Circle Backward

The straddle and half-sole circle backward is a preliminary exercise for many advanced bar movements. It is usually taught in the first instance as a dismount, first from the low bar and then progressing to the high bar. Start from a straddle position, hips high and feet close to the hands, maintaining complete balance over the bar so that the hands can slip forward slightly, grasping underneath the bar. Drop backwards, keeping the arms very straight and pulling strongly on the hands, with the hips and knees pressing backwards and feet pressed into the bar. When the hips have passed underneath the bar but are still rising, release the feet, bring the legs quickly together and dismount or half-turn.

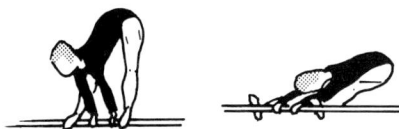

backwards until the hips have passed underneath the bar and are rising upwards. Keep the feet moving towards the high bar, release the low bar and grasp the high bar in a long hang.
This movement can also be performed with a half-turn to catch the high bar. *See below.*

Variations on the Sole Circle

Stand on the low bar, facing the high bar, either in a straddle position or with the feet together between the hands. Circle

81

Sole Circle Forward

Start in a straddle position or with feet together, knees straight and hands in a reverse grip. Fall forward, pressing the feet into the bar. Natural swing will take you well underneath the bar, when you can either release hands and feet, re-catch the low bar and move to long swing and upstart or follow the movement in an upward direction to catch the high bar.

Sole circle forward

Progression to catch the high bar

Squat and Straddle Movements

The majority of bar routines, whatever the standard, have as part of their content squat or straddle movements, and complete mastery of these movements will always be to the advantage of the gymnast.

In these movements there is a high backward swing, as in the backward circle, and the hips remain high as the legs squat either onto the bar or between the hands to a sitting position. In the straddle movement the legs should not be wide but arrive on the bar close to the hands. The shoulders play a part in maintaining balance in both movements, being forward at the start of the movement but pulling the back slightly to adjust the balance on completion of the movement.

Swinging Movements

Preparatory swinging movements can be learned at a very early stage in training. The following suggestions will not only help form the swing for the future but will assist the young gymnast in experiencing timing and gaining confidence on what appears to a small beginner to be a rather large piece of equipment:

- Jump backwards into a piked hang, hands in a regular grip on the low bar, and move through a long underswing, returning to a standing position.
- Starting in a front support position on the low bar, swing the legs forward slightly, swing backwards and lift away from the bar to a horizontal position, keeping the shoulders over the bar (layout). Return to the bar and repeat. Many repetitions of this, keeping the body tight and straight and aiming to go above the horizontal, will result in a much smoother, more continuous exercise in the future. This movement is rarely practised sufficiently and it is of the utmost importance in the composition of a first-class bar routine. Practise repetitions of backward circles with a high layout without stops in between circles.

- As above, prepare for a high layout, but instead of returning to the bar push away with the hands to land on the floor. This can then be performed with a half or full turn and eventually transferred to the high bar.
- To feel the shape of the backward swing in preparation for the backward seat circle and the single and double leg uprise, sit on the bar in a back support position, lift clear of the bar, drop back and on the return swing push the legs through the arms to land on the floor.
- Although the high bar is not used for young gymnasts in the first instance, they can be allowed to swing backwards and forwards on this bar, learning to keep a straight and tight body and finding a good rhythm. If there is any fear of the height of the bar, this will help to overcome it.

Long Swing from High Bar

From a front support position on the high bar swing the legs forward and on the return swing push upwards and backwards with the arms, allowing the body to swing down to a long hang and swing in towards the low bar.

Arms and body should be tight and straight; there should be no hollow or pike as this will result in the gymnast hitting the low bar in the wrong position. When learning this movement, the gymnast must be put through the correct position on the low bar. When the movement is transferred to the high bar, to assist the gymnast to feel the correct position the coach can hold the pupil's feet and lower her through the arm position to a long hand *(see left)*.

There is a great tendency with this movement to throw very fast with bent arms and a hollow back, but if the feet are held the gymnast not only has to use her arms but also will not be able to throw her feet too high.

When a gymnast attempts this movement for the first time alone, it is advisable to cover the low bar with a mat or have supporters to slow her down as she approaches the low bar. From a safety point of view the gymnast should be taught as early as possible to pike her legs quickly when her hips hit the bar.

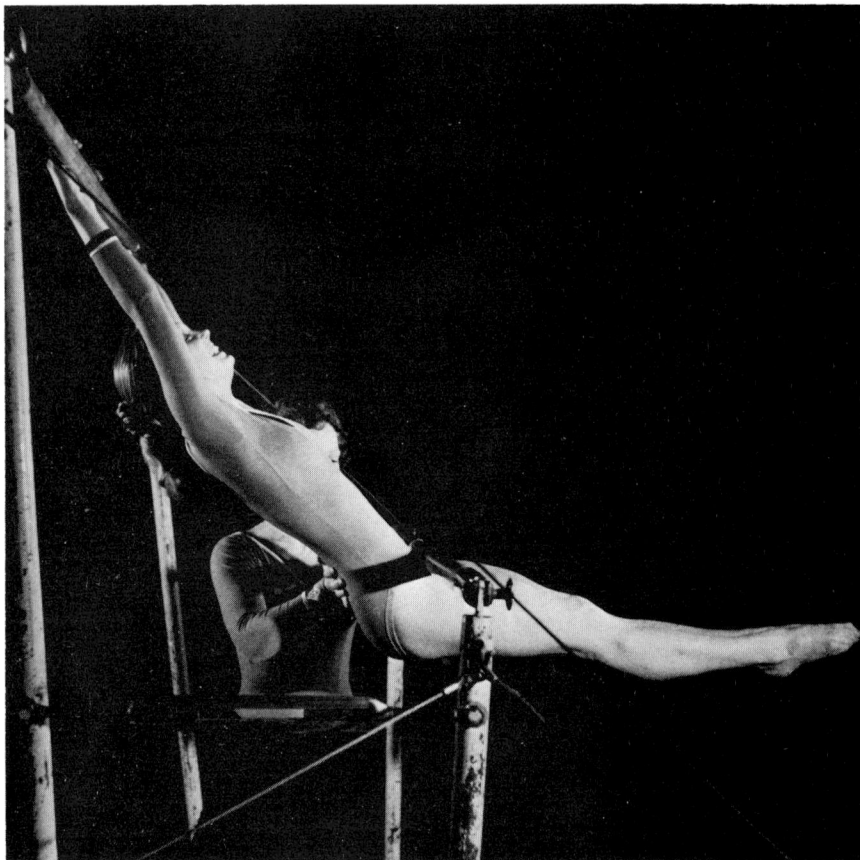

Measuring the distance between the bars to ensure that the gymnast meets the low bar at hip level

Long Swing and Backward Hip Circle of Low Bar

When the hips come into contact with the low bar after the long swing, the legs immediately pike round the bar with the bar held in the hips. As you feel the pull on your arms, release your hold on the high bar and transfer your hands to the low bar, by which time the legs will have continued circling the bar, and with a lift of the upper body reach the front support position.

This movement requires support until it is truly mastered as there is a danger of the gymnast releasing her grasp of the high bar too soon.

The long swing may also be performed from a front support position on the high bar, facing outwards. The long swing then takes place over the low bar, the hips beating the low bar while the hands retain their grip on the high bar, to be followed on the return swing by a squat on or over the low bar or a straddle over. Alternatively, release the high bar, catch the low bar in pike position and do a long underswing.

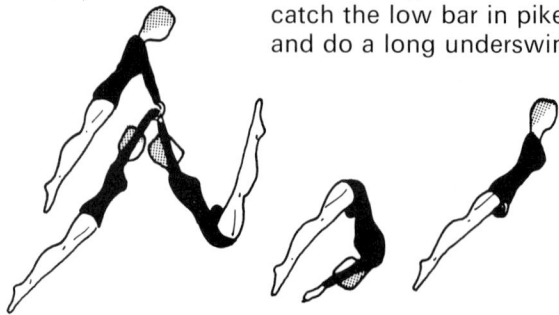

Gymnasts should not attempt this or any other movement which beats or wraps the bar if they are not tall enough to hit the bar at hip level.

Half-turn Long Swing and Backward Hip Circle

To feel the body position of the half-turn, the gymnast should sit on the low bar facing the high bar, with hands on high bar. The coach, holding both the gymnast's feet, pulls her out to hang in full stretched position on the high bar. At the end of the extension, the gymnast makes a half-turn by releasing one hand and swings into the low bar, with the hands in a mixed grip.

The second step is to let the gymnast make the turn herself, either from sitting on the low bar or from a squat position. The feet must be directed upwards and the turn made at the end of the swing. Difficulty will be experienced in lifting the feet in the first instance, and support from the hips will assist.

Alternative starting positions for the half-turn are:

- From a front rest position on the high bar drop back, passing through a 'V' sit position, and shoot the legs out to make a half-turn.
- From a straddle on or over the high bar, drop back underneath the bar and make a half-turn to a long swing.

The straddle on half-turn is probably the easiest method, as the feet are already high when coming out of the straddle and are in a good position to shoot into the half-turn.

Straddle half-turn long swing

The straddle half-turn should eventually be achieved with a complete release of both hands to re-catch the high bar so that both hands are in a regular grip. However, it is advisable to master the straddle on and half-turn with one hand released first, as the turn and re-catch with two hands must be made at the height of the swing when the body weight is negligible and the body has not started to drop below the bar, making the re-catch difficult.

The double hand change is a necessary progression as it keeps the movement in the centre of the bars.

The straddle half-turn can also be performed from a straddle on the high bar, facing the low bar. This means that the half-turn takes place above the low bar and the beat of the hips against the low bar will take place much earlier. It is therefore important that some protection is used on the low bar for learning purposes and that the bars, as in all these wrap movements, are the required distance apart for each gymnast. Upon hitting the bar the legs will pike round it and immediately swing back into the next movement.

Dislocation Catch

The dislocation catch is a continuation of the long swing and backward hip circle to catch the high bar in a dislocation grip. The main difference apart from the grip is that the backward circle is performed without hands, leaving the arms free to reach quickly backwards into the dislocation grip on the high bar. Progressions leading to the dislocation catch are as follows:

- The following will help to familiarise gymnasts with the unusual dislocation grip. In this

85

Dislocation catch—note the method of support. See also that the hands of the gymnast are turning as she lifts from the low bar in preparation for the dislocation grip on the high bar

grip the hands are wider than the shoulders and are in reverse grip. Because of the width of the shoulders it is not easy to hang in this position, so it should be done for a short time only at first.

Standing underneath the high bar supporters, lift the gymnast into the dislocation hold. As confidence in the hold increases, make the jump to the bar quicker.

■ Practise the long swing with support without bringing the hands to the bar on the backward circle. When the pull on the hands on the high bar is felt and the legs are piked round the low bar, release the hands and circle the low bar, arms reaching towards the floor. As the circle continues, thrust the arms strongly upwards and backwards towards the high bar. At this stage you are merely attempting to complete the backward circle without the use of hands, not trying to catch the high bar.

■ Hang over the low bar at the hip joint, arms hanging downwards. With the coach holding your legs, practise lifting the arms and upper body as strongly as possible, reaching backwards to catch the high bar in a dislocation grip.

When the above points have been mastered, the whole movement should be possible, with support from the coach as in point 3. Particular attention should be given to the legs, which should not be allowed to rotate around the bar but should be held back as the arms and upper body are transferred to the high bar.

Dislocation catch

Straddle Cut to Long Hang

Sit in the back support position on the high bar, facing the low bar. Swing backwards to a half-inverted hang. On the return swing, keep the legs moving

Straddle cut to long hang

forward as if to return to a sitting position on the bar, but when the head and shoulders are above the bar release the hands momentarily to allow the legs to straddle past the arms. Re-grasp the bar, join the legs together and swing to a long hang.

The straddle cut can be learned first on the low bar, with the supporter standing behind the gymnast and holding her waist on the return swing, and on the high bar with a box horse, using the same support method.

Upstart Movements

Upstart from Low Bar to High Bar

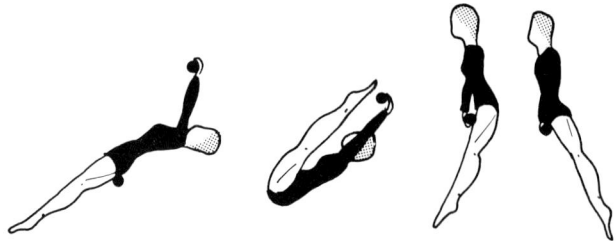

From a rear lying position, press the legs downward to give impetus to the upstart and pike the body sharply, bringing the toes back towards the bar. Keep the legs moving in an upward direction until the bar has passed the knees. Swing the legs downward, keeping the hips high, and as the body rises press on the hands, allowing the shoulders to rise above the bar.

Long Underswing Upstart to Catch High Bar

For a long underswing, see p. 76. At the end of the upstart, before the legs are swung backwards, push from the hands and transfer the weight to end in a long hang on the high bar.

Upstart from low bar to high bar

Long Upstart

The long upstart is more difficult than the previous upstarts as it commences from a long hang on the high bar. When learning this upstart, it is useful to break the movement into four parts as follows:

- From sitting on the low bar facing the high bar, hands on the high bar, drop to hang on the high bar with the feet pointing strongly to the ground and stomach leading on the swing forward.
- Pull strongly through the shoulders without allowing the shoulders to swing too far

forward, lifting the hips so that the body is in a horizontal position.
- Pike the legs back towards the bar as in previous upstarts.
- Rise above the bar as in previous upstarts.

If you count each movement through, it will cut the tendency to rush the movement, so making it difficult to rise above the bar on the last part.

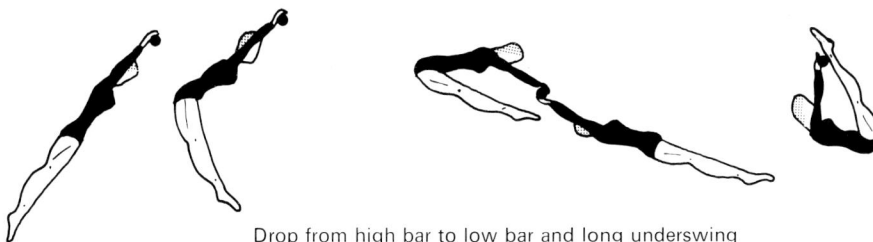

Drop from high bar to low bar and long underswing

Drop from High Bar to Low Bar and Long Underswing

It is necessary to perform the pike and long underswing competently before attempting the drop. To obtain the feel of movement from one bar to the other, hang on the high bar with support on either side. Pull the seat backwards, pulling on the bar with the hands, and drop to the low bar, holding the pike position. At first there will be a tendency to reach forward for the low bar too quickly, and the result will be bent arms and legs. It should be borne in mind that the body should be in the piked long underswing position when the hands connect with the low bar. If this is not so, there will not only be bent arms and legs but the underswing will be cut short, making the next movement difficult. At the commencement of the drop, when the body is lifting to the pike position, the seat should be behind the high bar. Progression from the drop from long hang would be to a drop from an inverted position on the high bar. From back-lying, take both legs straight through the arms to an inverted position, keeping the hips high, and drop to the low bar. You should be able to see the bar and the legs should be forward in the pike position, not pointing downwards, when the drop is made.

Drop from high bar in piked position to low bar and long underswing

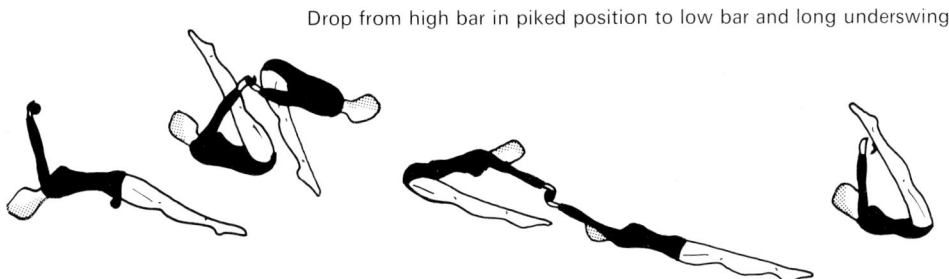

Back Urise

From the front support position on the high bar, make a long swing to pike the legs around the low bar. As the hips swing back under the bar pike slightly, pulling strongly with the arms to lift the body upwards into a front support position on the high bar.

This movement can also be performed from a front support position on the high bar facing outwards, swinging backwards over the low bar. Gymnasts may find this movement easier as they can make full use of the rebound from the low bar to assist the rise to the high bar.

Back uprise from and to front support position on the high bar, facing outwards

Twisting Elements

Half-turn from low bar to catch high bar

Full turn from low bar to catch high bar

There are many twisting elements on the asymmetric bars, but these should not be attempted until all the basic skills have been perfected.

The following elements can, however, be performed in safety, and will assist the more advanced twisting elements to be learned later.

Twists must be made quickly with a tight body, and must be fully completed before landing.

Full twist from front rest on high bar, to re-catch high bar

- Start in a front rest position on the high bar, facing the low bar. Lay-off the bar, thrusting from the hands, and make a half-turn to land on the mat.
- Lay-off the bar, thrusting from

the hands, and make a full turn to land on the mat.
- From a front rest position on the high bar, make a long swing and pike forcefully. Swing backwards, at the same time

Full twist from long swing to re-catch the high bar

pressing down on the bar to raise the body until the head is above the bar. Release your grip and make a half-turn to land on the mat.

Repeat, attempting a full turn, keeping your arms over your head.

Repeat, attempting a full turn to re-catch the high bar.

With plenty of crash mats this activity can be practised quite safely.

Do not attempt the advanced twisting moves without supervision. In the early stages it is essential for a gymnast to feel the twist herself; comments from the coach as to what she is doing wrong are invaluable, but if the coach is actually twisting her body for her it is difficult for the gymnast to know exactly what her body is doing.

Dismounts

Squat

Commence as for a squat through, but as the feet pass over the bar use your hands to push from the bar, keeping the upper body lifted. Land with a slight knee bend and body stretched.

Underswing from Low Bar

Start in a front support position on the low bar. Drop the shoulders back and lift the legs forward, giving a piked position in the hips. Allow the body to drop under the bar and, as the hands push away from the bar, shoot the legs upwards in an arch position. This movement can be done in a variety of ways, e.g. from the high bar facing outwards with a half or full twist; from the high bar facing inwards, the movement coming over the low bar with a half or full twist.

Underswing from high bar facing inwards

Straddle Undershoot

Start from a front rest position on the low bar, facing outwards. Do a layout straddle onto the bar with hands close to the feet (toes, not insteps, on the bar). The straddle must be firmly balanced on top of the bar so that the hands can be dropped slightly under the bar for a better grip. Pulling the stomach in and pressing the feet into the bar and the knees back, fall backwards under the bar until the legs reach an almost horizontal position. Then release the bar, bringing the legs together, and hollow off to land.

Straddle Cut

Learn as for the straddle cut to
long hang, making sure that the
cut is made whilst the body is in a
vertical position, head and
shoulders above the bar. If the cut
is made too early, while the body
is horizontal, this will result in the
gymnast falling on her back.

Learning the hecht

Hecht

Start in the front support position on the high bar, facing inwards. Make a long swing, as for a long swing backward hip circle without hands. Hold the piked position until a three-quarter hip circle has been completed, then reach upwards and forwards with the arms and upper body, at the same time lifting the legs. The momentum of the long swing and the movement of the body position from piked to straight will carry the body forward to land clear of the bar. There must be an even reaction of legs and upper body, as too much leg action and insufficient body action will result in a 'nose dive' onto the mat, and too much body lift upward with no forward action and no leg lift will not bring the body away from the low bar.
To learn the hecht, the gymnast

hangs over the low bar, with the bar in her hip. She should practise lifting from a pike to straight position many times. A mat over the bar will enable more repetitions to be made in the early stages.
Progress to supporters assisting the gymnast from this position through a hecht to land. Assistance must be given in clearing the legs, as well as keeping the upper body lifted. Progression can then be made to the full movement. Support can be given by a hand on the stomach of the gymnast before she has completed the long swing, thus giving her the assurance that support is there before the hecht movement is commenced. Until the gymnast has fully mastered the movement it is advisable for an additional supporter to be prepared for the legs not lifting by standing in between the bars.

a

b

c

f

g

h

The hecht from front support on the high bar, passing through long swing

Basic Routines

As continuity and stamina on the asymmetric bars are two of the most important requisites, it is advisable to have even the youngest member of the club doing movements in sequence. For obvious reasons very simple sequences should be used in the beginning, substituting a slightly more difficult movement as the gymnast progresses, but not until the first routine is perfect.

The following are suggested routines in two groups which could be used as gradual progressions to assist continuity and stamina, and which can be adapted to suit individual requirements. These beginner progressions are on the low bar only.

First Progression

a Hands on bar in regular grip
Half backward circle to front support
Push away to land.

b Half backward circle to front support from one foot
Backward circle
Push away to land.

c Half backward circle to front support from one foot
Backward circle
Single leg squat through
Half-turn and push away to land.

d Half backward circle to front support from one foot
Backward circle
Single leg squat through
Single leg uprise
Half-turn and push away to land.

e Half backward circle from two feet
Backward circle
Single leg squat through
Single leg uprise
Half-turn and push away to land.

f Half backward circle from two feet
Backward circle
Single leg squat through
Single leg uprise
Half-turn
Squat two feet over the bar to land.

Second Progression

a Long underswing and upstart
Push away to land.

b Long underswing and upstart
Backward circle
Push away to land.

c Long underswing and upstart
Backward circle
Straddle on sole circle backwards to dismount.

d Long underswing and upstart
Backward circle
Squat two feet between hands
Half-turn to front rest
Straddle on sole circle backwards to dismount.

e Long underswing and upstart
Backward circle
Squat two feet between hands
Two-legged uprise
Half-turn to front rest
Straddle on sole circle to dismount.

f Long underswing and upstart
Forward circle
Squat two feet between hands
Two-legged uprise
Half-turn to front rest
Straddle on sole circuit to dismount.

The sequences can be extended in this manner to include both bars, to any standard required. In this way every gymnast can be performing a continuous exercise adapted to her own ability.

Vault

It is often wrongly assumed that because the vault is over very quickly it does not require as much attention as the other three pieces of apparatus used in women's gymnastics. In fact, the same mark of 10 is awarded for all four pieces and the vault must be given a great deal of attention as the gymnast has only seconds to gain as many marks as possible.

There are various ways of helping young gymnasts to run naturally in preparation for the vault, i.e. running races, running at speed to jump onto crash mats, running around the gym and outside for stamina and running short bursts of speed measured to the approximate length of a vaulting run. A natural run should be encouraged, on the balls of the feet, elbows bent and weight slightly forward. Try very early on in training to cut out extra hops and skips both at the start and in the middle of the run.

Although in competition the horse is always used, you will find that for development purposes a great deal of advantage can be gained from using a box horse, particularly with a large class, when a box placed at any height can be used for take-off, landing, etc. This sometimes gives confidence to the young gymnast who feels afraid of running at speed towards a horse with space underneath.

The use of the box horse in the following manner for learning a vault of any grade of difficulty will create a safe situation, ensuring that gymnasts are competent and fully understand the various stages of the vault before transferring to the horse and performing the complete vault.

1. When the gymnast has learned to use the spring-board, place a low box sideways behind the board and practise the squat and straddle onto the top of the box.

2. Squat onto the box and immediately make a high jump upwards with feet together, to land on the mat. This combines board take-off, squat position and landing practice.

3. Place the box longways, squat on, reach immediately for the end and squat to the mat *(below)*.

The gymnast must prepare to perform the squat vault with the spring-board some distance away from the horse. This method of practising the squat on a horse placed longways gives the feeling of the extended body position before the squat takes place.

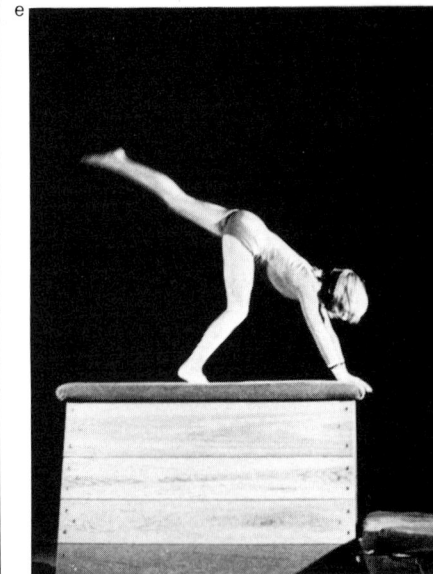

4. Place the box longways, and prepare for landing from the handspring vault. Squat on and handspring with support, pushing from the hands with a straight body to turn over and land on the mat. The height of the box for this type of exercise depends on the height of the gymnast. Tall girls will need a higher box. *See the sequence below.*

5. Repeat no. 4 but perform a cartwheel sideways to land on two feet in preparation for the cartwheel vault. Use this situation to learn the push from the hands and the complete sideways wheel with the body tight.

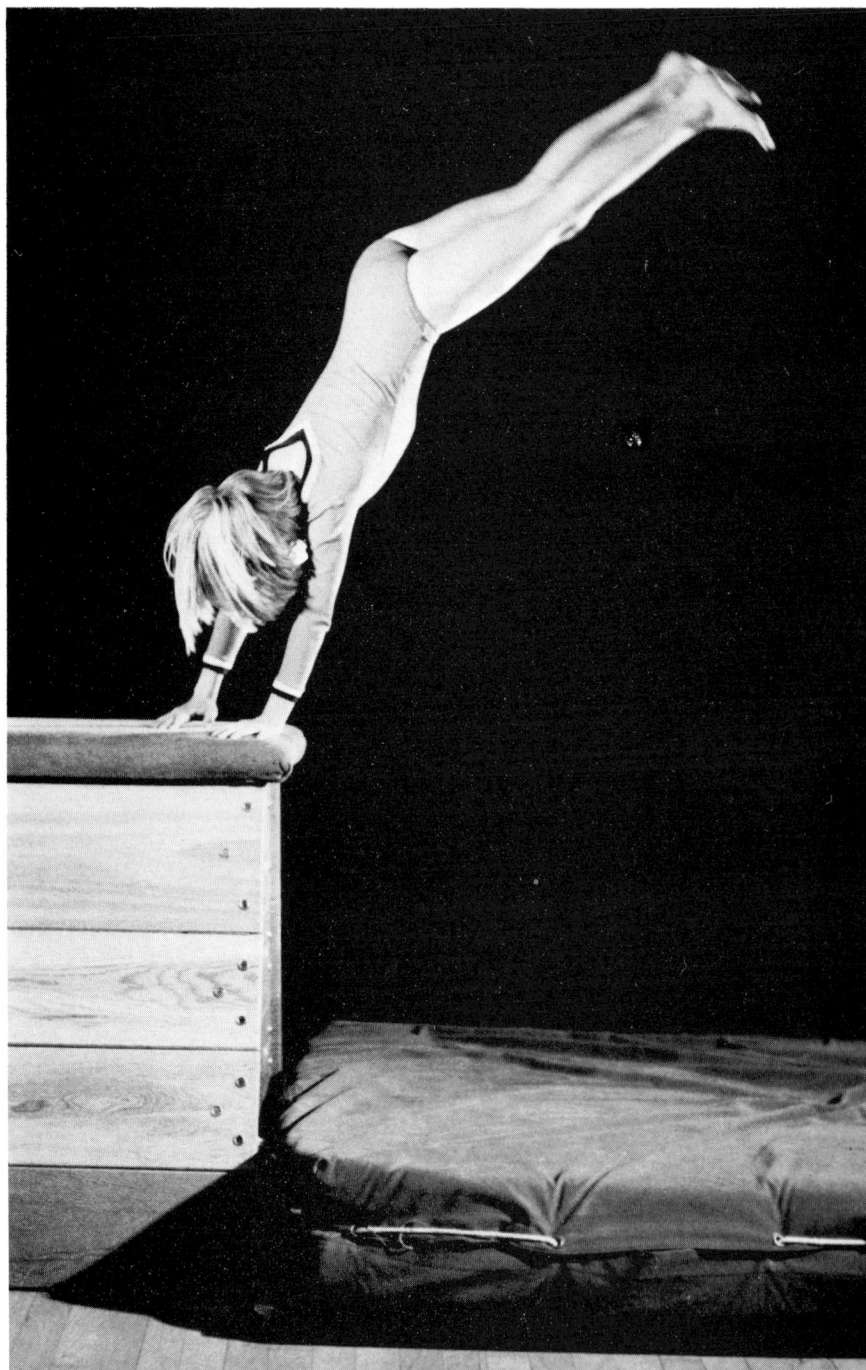

Beginners will gain confidence for the cartwheel vault by performing a round-off from the end of the horse

6. To assist the first flight in an inverted vault, dive onto a crash mat to obtain the feeling of the upward jump with body stretched and the rise of the heels without piking or hollowing. *See left.*

7. Starting with a low box placed sideways and using the spring-board, transfer no. 6 to this situation. With the box low, gymnasts will feel the flight onto the horse. Do not have the board too close to the box as the body must be stretched before landing on the horse. Always have support at both sides of the horse and a crash mat on which to land when learning this vault. If each stage of the vault is mastered before moving to the next stage the support also can be lessened, but it is dangerous to progress too quickly as each part of the vault must be fully understood by the individual gymnast.

Preparation for the cartwheel vault

Gaining confidence for the first flight

8. To improve the first flight of the vertical vaults, place the horse longways and perform the handspring over the full length of the box.

Coaches should remember that when classes are divided into groups the vaulting section will tire more quickly, and take-off and landing practice should be organised as a break from the vault.

The Run and Take-off

Practise jumping on the spring-
board only at first until you have
mastered the single leg take-off to
land on the board with two feet.
Then join run and take-off
together, to land on crash mats.
Strive for a consistent powerful
run which does not slow down as
you approach the spring-board.
Do not run with the head down;
focus on the horse.
If there is a problem landing on
the board in the correct place, use
a chalk mark as a guide.
If a slow run is a problem, the
gymnast can be timed to
encourage her to run faster.
Alternatively, a faster gymnast can
run with her.
The last step will be a big one—
bringing the feet together to strike
the spring-board, knees in front of
shoulders, to gain upward
momentum for vertical vaults, e.g.
handstand and cartwheel.
At the commencement of the last
step swing both arms backward,
join the feet together in
preparation for take-off, and swing
both arms forward to the vertical.
The arms are on the way up the
front when you jump onto the
spring-board. The arm action of
individual gymnasts upon hitting
the board does vary, and if a
particular gymnast has problems
with the general approach then it
should be changed to suit her
needs as long as the technique of

the vault is not affected.

The distance of the spring-board from the horse depends upon the ability of the performer. A beginner will probably start with the board fairly close to the horse and increase the distance at the discretion of the coach, on improvement of confidence and ability. Body tension is extremely important in the vault from the moment the gymnast strikes the spring-board, and in fact can be the difference between a top quality vault and a mediocre one.

First Flight

The first flight is the extension of the take-off jump until the moment the hands touch the horse. A good first flight cannot be accomplished with the spring-board too near the horse. The abdominal muscles must be pulled in and the hips lifted high. There must be no pike and no hollow in the back. For the vertical vaults, the arms must be high but not behind the ears. The heels must rise fast but this must be combined with abdominal tension or the back will hollow. The coach is not allowed to stand in between the spring-board and the horse to assist the first flight during competition, but in some cases it may be necessary and helpful in the early learning stages to assist the gymnast to feel the correct body position for a vertical vault.

Landing on the Horse

The actual landing on the horse for any vault is momentary. The arms must be straight, hands flat, fingers forwards and arms shoulder-width apart (hands too wide cannot push off). The gymnast must be mentally prepared for immediate action upon hitting the horse, for the push-off into the second flight.

Second Flight

The aim of the second flight is to equal the distance of the first flight. The push-off into the second flight should be achieved not by bending the arms but by pushing from the hands and extending through the shoulders. If the spring-board is too far away for the ability of the gymnast a good second flight will not be possible. If the vault is slow the same result will occur.

Landing

The bad landing of a vault, with resulting loss of marks, is one of the most common faults in competitive gymnastics. Landings from boxes, etc. must be practised at every vaulting session. The arrival onto the mat after a vault at speed is a shock to the system which must be absorbed first by the toes, then the heels, then the

knees, which must bend. Landings with flat feet and straight knees will cause injury.

The arms can be of great benefit in maintaining the balance on landing; keep them up or raise them before the knees have straightened.

The necessity for a good second flight shows in the landing; if the body is leaning forward through lack of flight the landing will be unsuccessful.

Horizontal Vaults

Squat

From take-off the arms reach forward and the body is almost horizontal and straight. The legs must not be above the horizontal. The knees are tucked up to the arms, not taken through them, when passing over the horse, but must straighten to land. A fast strong upward thrust from the hands will assist the forward flight and straighten the body for landing. If there is no push from the hands and the shoulders are forward, the body will over-rotate on landing.

Straddle

Approach as for the squat, keeping the legs in the almost horizontal position until the hands are on the horse. The straddle occurs with the push-off from the hands and does not come straight from the board. After the push-off, the legs must close and the body straighten quickly to land.

The above vaults can also be performed with the addition of a high layout above horizontal at the take-off point.

Vertical Vaults

Handspring

This vault is the basis of all vertical vaults, and must therefore be given a great deal of attention in the learning stages. As the gymnast progresses from horizontal to vertical vaults, it is necessary to change the direction of the jump from forwards to upwards. Coaches can assist by standing behind the spring-board and supporting the gymnast in the jump. When the correct direction of the jump has been achieved, to assist the first flight a high dive roll can be made over a rope onto a thick mat, paying attention to the lift of the heels and the tension required to keep the body straight. Progressions are then made to the low box and, as confidence and ability increase, the box is heightened, the distance of the board increased, and support reduced. Always allow the gymnast to absorb the preceding step before moving to the next stage. The time taken over learning the handspring vault will speed up considerably the achievement of much higher tariff vaults.

Cartwheel

Approach as for the handspring with a two-foot take-off and upward jump, making a quarter turn during the first flight to land sideways on the horse.

The hands are placed on the horse one after the other, and there must be a good thrust from both hands to ensure any second flight. The vault must hit the centre of the horse with the quarter turn completed before the hands are placed.

Cartwheel

Cartwheel with half-turn

Yamashita

Yamashita half-turn

The approach is as for the handspring but the hips are pressed down in the first flight, making this a flatter flight. As the hands make contact with the horse, keep the feet and legs moving upwards and push strongly from the hands, allowing the trunk to catch up with the legs to show a free 'V' sit position. Keeping the arms high, extend the hips to land with the body leaning slightly backwards. The second flight will be higher and shorter than the first flight.

Yamashita

Conclusion

The most successful gymnasts are the ones who are able to give their very best performances during competition, whether it be local, national or international competition. It is a symbol of dedication when a gymnast is able to recover quickly, both mentally and physically, from any mistake she may make.

The degree of concentration required on apparatus cannot be emphasised too strongly, particularly as most competitions are held simultaneously on all four pieces of apparatus. For example, the music accompanying the floor exercise can be disturbing to competitors on the vault, beam and bars.

Furthermore, as the exercise for each piece of apparatus lasts for a different period of time, applause for one competitor can disturb the concentration of a competitor on another piece.

It is therefore most important that gymnasts learn the powers of concentration in the early stages of their training so that they are able to perform creditably in any situation. An early adaption to the competitive situation can be achieved by club competitions, to be followed later by local, regional and national competitions. The British Amateur Gymnastics Association control gymnastics in Great Britain and they have an excellent development plan for girls which is used regionally and nationally. This plan is specially devised to take gymnasts through basic gymnastics to international standard competitively, and anyone wishing to take up the sport of gymnastics is advised to follow this comprehensive plan.